DAY TRADING

Your Millionaire Guide

A Beginner's Guide To Day Trading, You'll Learn How To Make a Living and Use the Best Trading Tools, Money Management and Advanced Techniques to Make Money

TABLE OF CONTENTS

INTRODUCTION

There are people who, thanks to trading, have changed their lives and that of many people who have believed in them. It is enough to mention the name of Warren Buffet or George Soros because dreams and visions begin to start in the minds of many traders.

Trading success is achieved by staying very down to earth.

Starting from this belief, I have written this manual in a simple way with the aim of helping newbies to find the right way to be successful, but, above all, to find the right methods to avoid losing money, which are usually saved with sacrifice.

Trading is not synonymous with gambling. Trading on the financial markets is neither a game nor a hobby. Your approach must be extremely serious and disciplined, you have to pay particular attention to safeguarding the capital you decide to invest. Being aware of your personality, your fears, your goals you can use this to your advantage, making it your secret weapon.

CHAPTER ONE
WHAT IS DAY TRADING

What is day trading?

When we talk about day trading we mean a way of trading in the markets with trades that open and close on the same day. Those who do this type of trading tend not to have positions held overnight, but they try to close them every night and reopen them the next day. Day trading is a short term strategy that aims to profit from small intraday price fluctuations rather than longer term market movements.

When we talk about day trading we refer to a way of trading in the markets with trades that open and close on the same day.

The meaning of day trading is in direct contrast to traditional investment techniques that involve buying at a low cost, holding and then selling at a high cost. Day traders must therefore think differently from investors, focusing on the price action of an asset rather than its long-term potential. This is why day trading strategies tend to use a lot of different technical analysis solutions and require the trader to stay up to date with the latest news.

Pros of day trading

There are many markets on which day traders can operate: futures, stocks, forex and commodities. Stocks are very popular because they allow you to eliminate the risk of gapping overnight markets by being able to close them at the end of each day. The rise of technology in recent years has definitely made this way of trading more and more popular.

Cons of day trading

Day trading is not for the part-time trader. It requires concentration and dedication, as it involves quick decisions and the execution of a large number of operations in a single day. Day traders don't necessarily have to trade all day, but they need to stay alert and stay ahead of the markets. Day traders can be limited by the resulting costs. For example, if you buy and sell stocks you will pay a commission. As with all types of trading, day trading carries a market risk which can be substantial when using leveraged instruments.

CHAPTER TWO
PSYCHOLOGY
AND MINDSET

Trading errors

In Gann's theory the psychological aspect is of great importance. The volatility and unpredictability of the financial markets require traders to have steady nerves and continuous critical analysis of their actions. Among the mistakes that are most frequently committed by operators, emotion is the most recurrent; dominating fear, hope and greed is the first task that every good trader should set himself.

Basing one's speculative actions on the evidence of the facts is only possible by creating a trading plan before operating, since hope or expectations manifest themselves with such fascination as to mislead even the best trader; acting in accordance with rumors or on the basis of false hopes is unfortunately a recurring behavior, which often leads to even bearing large losses before closing the position. According to Gann, a healthy fear of the market is the first sign that reveals the potential of the successful trader. Speculating is a business where losses are inevitable and physiological to a certain extent. The trader who monetizes a loss after a speculation and doesn't get too excited is mature enough to do his job. The feeling of fear, which must be avoided, greed, or the desire to improve one's position, is another personal aspect that must be mastered. Greed stimulates emotion and this can lead the operator to hope that the

market will still see his expectations and may also be induced to make investments for an amount not justified by good money management rules. Therefore, to have a logical rather than an emotional approach, it is necessary to prepare in advance an operational plan or trading plan that allows us to fix exactly the operations we want to do. According to Gann, the most important thing to do, when drawing up an operational plan, is to set stop-loss signals or to set price levels, beyond which a "coherent" buy or sell order is given.

Equally important is that the trader does not try to tell others what he is speculating on. This behavior, in fact, can only lead him to increase self-esteem and convince him, even more, that he is on the right side of the market, thus feeding his hopes on the price list rather than on predictive analysis on quotes. Gann advised buying when bad news arrived and selling when good news came in, which could prove to be unfounded.

The trader should behave independently, this means that he should develop his beliefs only after carefully studying the markets, without following the advice of others. In drawing up an operational plan, an accretive type process should always be followed, increasing positions on a financial asset only after it has already provided earnings.

If the speculations are made by two people, Gann recommends dividing the tasks as follows: the one should set the buying and selling times while the other should identify the levels around which to set the stop-loss. The operational plan is essential in order not to suffer a type of emotional behavior when operating in the financial markets. Obviously, once the trading plan has been drawn up, it is essential to follow it without being misled by emotional factors, as we have already said. Speculating is a profession where losses are inevitable and to some extent functional.

Therefore, drawing up a trading plan is necessary to have a logical approach, rather than an emotional one; being able to eliminate the intrinsic emotionality of trading is almost impossible, but it is certainly the right way to follow.

Beware about your decisions

Discipline is one of the most important elements that experienced traders have in common. Keep an eye on your bad habits and try to solve them as soon as possible. Trade in a disciplined manner if you decide to establish a carefully thought-out set of rules to govern your trading decisions, and then stick to them. Find ways to avoid breaking your rules and try to solve every problem before it becomes one!

Also, as a day trader, it is a good idea to reevaluate your rules at the end of each month, due to the shorter lead times of this style of trading.

But there are sources of inspiration that you should follow in order to arrive at the expected results more effectively.

Money management

Money management is essential in day trading although, ultimately, it is one of the essential elements of trading in any investment time frame. Of course, if you intend to trade for many years to come, you will need to apply successful money management strategies. There are entire books devoted to this subject, which contain many different approaches, and you need to take the time to find a method that you are comfortable with.

The risk / reward ratio is important. Remember: it doesn't matter to make a profit 90% of the time if your losses are much larger than your wins. What is important is that your wins are greater than your losses.

Stop loss

Never forget to use stop losses to manage risk when placing your orders to enter the market. This is your main "insurance": you must be aware that these should be the most important elements when opening a new position, as they will protect you from operations that evolve in a different way than expected. Standard stop losses may be subject to slippage when price gapping occurs, however, guaranteed stop losses will always close positions at your chosen level.

Determine your best strategy

No strategy always works, but even a simple day trading strategy can help a trader try to spot low-risk, high-yielding trades at important points in the day. Some traders would also use the failure of a trade as an opportunity to set up another. Should the level be "broken", it can signal the start of a new trend, presenting another opportunity to try to make money.

Controlling emotions in online trading

Mindfulness means "conscious attention" and is "a way of focusing attention on the present moment, paying attention to your thoughts, your emotions and the signals that your body sends you the moment they occur, observing them without prejudice ".

Mindfulness

In fact, Mindfulness is not a kind of religion or spiritual practice, it is simply a form of "Training the Mind". Even the Marines use it: they call it "Mind Fitness".

Equanimity and Impermanence are the two fundamental principles underlying Mindfulness. Don't be fooled by big words, they are much simpler and more intuitive than you imagine.

Equanimity is about accepting your every thought, emotion, every impulse or feeling, without trying to suppress them or resist them. Mind you: Equanimity does not mean resignation. Equanimity does not push you to give up in the face of reality, rather it helps you to observe it for what it really is, allowing you to act accordingly. The principle of Impermanence teaches that everything around you is in a perpetual state of change.

Financial markets, for example, are uncertain and always changing. You can't do anything about it, that's their nature.

By accepting the markets for what they are, you will be able to ease your "performance anxiety": to be clear, that anxiety that pushes you to remain with an open position even when the market is clearly communicating that the time has come to close it.

How to manage information

In addition to performance anxiety, another great challenge that every trader often faces during his trading day is undoubtedly having to manage a huge load of information from all over the world.

Charts, indicators, latest news, economic calendar, etc., in short, you know what I'm talking about. In these situations of enormous pressure and confusion, Mindfulness will help you choose the most important information to focus on with extreme clarity, greatly reducing stress and improving your performance.

Self-awareness is the ability to step outside oneself and begin observing oneself from the point of view of an external and impartial spectator. By becoming aware of yourself, you will be able to get out of the flow of automatic actions you take without even thinking about it, and you will begin to direct your attention and energies according to your will.

While you are trading, where do you put your attention? On the results you are getting (Profits & Losses) or on your Trading System? In trading, the best decisions are made when focusing on the Trading System rather than the results obtained, as by focusing solely on the results, your future expectations and how much you think you will gain / lose from your positions, you will fall back into that performance anxiety. I was telling you about earlier.

If, on the other hand, you turn all your attention and all your energies on the development and improvement of your Trading System, you will avoid sleepless nights and anxieties of all kinds, and the results (profits) you will get will amaze you! Van Tharp, a legendary trader, used to say that: "You don't trade according to the market, you trade according to your beliefs about the market." It is extremely important, therefore, to recognize what your beliefs and convictions are. regarding financial markets and trading in general, because only in this way will you be able to understand the reason for your behavior and your reactions in front of the monitors.

The first step to trading more effectively is to become aware of your thoughts and everything that goes through your head when trading the markets. The key concept to understand here is that you are not your thoughts. Thoughts are only the fruit of the incessant work of our mind, they are not reality.

That said, none of us are able to choose the thoughts that go through their heads, but we can choose:

- how much attention to devote to each thought;
- what meaning to attribute to each thought.

Mistakes to avoid in online trading

One of the mistakes that can cost us dearly in the markets is to emotionally attach ourselves to any thought, for example: "I am holding the long position on EUR / USD open because I am sure the Euro will appreciate". In fact, this strong attachment risks hindering us from observing reality for what it is, and does not allow us to realize that perhaps the time has come to close.

Most traders, including professionals, have a secret dream: trading without the interference of emotions. In fact, we often perceive the emotional impact on our decisions as negative and detrimental to our performance. In reality, emotion is not only a key element of our decision-making process, but it is also the first element of every decision, because we first feel and then think.

Emotions provide us with messages about what we are experiencing, and as such, they are valuable data on which we can rely to direct our actions. Therefore, our goal should not be to be able to trade without emotions, precisely because we will only get better performance when we start trading taking into account our emotions. Instead of suppressing or ignoring the messages transmitted by our emotions, it is essential to learn how to manage them.

The first step in learning how to manage your emotions is simply to start feeling them.

How to manage the impulses

A sudden urge or desire to act. "The impulses we feel during our trading days can be of various types:

the urge to close the position too early to pocket the profit;

the urge to risk more than usual;

the urge to stay in front of the screen all day for fear of missing the right opportunity.

Being irrational reactions of the mind, impulses and sudden stimuli to act are very dangerous for our trading and the only way to follow to manage them is to "ride the wave". In fact, the impulses to act are like the waves of the sea: they come and go, they don't last forever.

Riding the wave therefore means observing the arrival of the impulse, accepting the impulse for what it is. By continuing to observe the impulse without following it, you will notice that its "impact force" will decrease until it disappears. And the more you train yourself to ride the waves of your irrational impulses, the less vehement will be the future waves that will hit you. By practicing Mindfulness, you will also gain greater control over your behaviors and you will be able to resist impulses, inhibiting them without too much effort.

Manage insights

Intuition is not something mystical or magical, it is simply a process that our mind uses to make future decisions using the information it has gathered in the past. An event experienced in the past, very often re-emerges in the form of a body signal: George Soros, for example, when he experiences severe back pain, interprets it as a signal that something is about to go wrong in his portfolio of securities. Therefore, when making trading decisions, logical reasoning alone is not enough: before deciding if something is good you should also listen to what your body communicates to you.

It is also true that making any decision involves a considerable expenditure of mental energy, and this "decision fatigue" has an extremely negative impact on the decisions you make every day.

To make intelligent decisions in line with your long-term goals, it will be useful to keep an eye on these 4 aspects:

- The sleep. Scientific studies show that sleeping a few hours a night leads to less feeling the weight of losses, and at the same time pushes to over-emphasize the positive results (in trading: profits).

- Exercise. Exercise increases the oxygenation of the brain, and this helps our mind to think more clearly.

- Food. Scientists recommend starting each day with a large breakfast, then continuing to eat at regular intervals to better manage your insulin and glucose supplies.

- Rest and Recovery. Alternate 90 minutes of trading with 20 minutes of recovery (i.e. leisure).

Manage your habits

Most of the actions that we repeat constantly and prolonged over time soon become a habit, that is an automatic behavior that we adopt unconsciously, and that we can only modify through a conscious effort. A habit, therefore, is "cemented" through the repetition of the same action over time, a repetition that develops new neural pathways in the brain that help you perform that specific action almost effortlessly.

However, it is very likely that over time we have automated behavior that is no longer useful or even harmful to our performance in the markets.

It usually works like this: in the past you have developed one or more habits in your way of trading for the sole reason that in that market moment those habits have made you a lot of money. As you know, however, financial markets are constantly evolving, and what was useful and profitable in the past may no longer be, today or in the near future.

I advise you to start observing your trading habits carefully, so as to identify and stop any counterproductive behavior. Use Mindfulness! As you practice the Mindfulness exercises I illustrated above, you will develop a greater awareness of your behaviors and your "automatic responses" to external events, and you will therefore also notice a series of habits that hinder your decisions and your performance on markets. After you become aware of your "bad habits", be very careful to replace them with new habits that are more effective for your trading.

Manage stress

Imagine this scene: you are in front of your PC and wait for the data on the American GDP to betray the news. The news comes out and the market begins to react: your heartbeats increase, your stomach contracts and your muscles tighten. The amygdala has just activated your stress response. You must know that each of us responds to stress in a different way, each of us experiences stress in different situations. This is because stress is not an external factor: stress is a perception and, as such, it is different for each individual. The external event can also be the same, but if this event will be perceived as a risk, it will determine in us a certain type of reaction, if instead the same event will be perceived as an opportunity, it will determine a totally different reaction.

Our performance will be poor both if we perceive too little stress and if we perceive too much of it. The optimal stress level for our performance is in fact a middle ground between little stress and too much stress, and we reach this optimal state every time the energies and efforts required by the market coincide with our ability to deal with it.

To feel the level of stress you are experiencing in the present moment, listen to your body: put your attention on the area between the chest and the abdomen: usually the stress is felt there. As soon as you have identified the area of your body that is most sensitive to stress, let this become your "Stress Barometer". By constantly placing your attention on this area, you will soon become more aware of your stress level and learn to manage it better.

Stress is an indispensable factor for our growth: by constantly pushing ourselves beyond our limits, it allows us to fully develop our potential. In order to avoid turning this precious ally into our worst enemy, however, we must always keep in mind the so-called "oscillation process". The "swing process" consists of alternating each period of stress with a period of rest and recovery. In fact, the problem for many of us is not too much stress, but the absence of recovery periods.

Physical resistance of the trader

Closely related to the concept of stress, is the concept of resilience. Resilience is defined as "the ability to recover quickly from times of difficulty", and can increase or decrease in the same way that the muscles in our body grow and shrink: with training.

The more we expose ourselves to difficult situations, the more our resilience muscle grows and strengthens. Furthermore, Jon Kabat-Zinn, the father of Mindfulness, has promoted several scientific researches aimed at measuring the impact of Mindfulness on resilience. From the studies carried out, it clearly emerges that Mindfulness significantly increases the level of resilience in individuals who practice it.

The importance of being patient

Trading is a way to make money. For some, it will be a business, for some a game. What you cannot forget is that emotions play an important role in life and also in business. And a very important skill that every trader should master is to have patience.

Some are more patient than others. Some people tend to speed things up. They want to know everything at once, they rush to trade different goods, use new indicators and open transactions. Others prefer to have a solid foundation, read and learn, try the features one by one, and be prepared when they finally enter the business.

If you are part of the first group, you don't have to worry. Patience is a skill. It is something you can learn through practice.

To put it plainly, patience is the ability to wait. Sit back and see what is happening on the chart. Analyze and wait. Wait for the right signals, wait for the right time to enter a position and then wait a little longer to see how the market is developing.

Patience is something you can learn

You already know that patience is something that can be learned. You are probably wondering now how to do this if it is not in your nature. You can do something as simple but effective as writing a short note for yourself. It could be "Be patient" or "Patience" or just "Wait". Put it in a visible place. You can even paste it directly into the trading image so that it is there every time you trade on your platform.

Waiting for trade can be tedious

Familiarize yourself with different trading strategies. Invest your time in learning how they work. You may be interested, for example, in how to combine RSI with support/resistance to create a powerful strategy. When choosing a strategy, stick to it. Don't be discouraged even if the signs to enter haven't appeared for a long time. Eventually they will.

Long wait for a good entry point

You wake up, sit down at your computer and log into your account. Choose the EUR/USD currency pair, set the Japanese candlestick table and 5 minute time candles. After this you need to add the indicators. However, it is important to remember that too many indicators could increase the chaos on your chart. The levels of support/resistance in combination with the RSI indicator would be sufficient.

Grab your coffee and wait. You are looking for the places where the price touches the support/resistance level and there is a divergence showing the RSI Indicator.

Waiting for the right opportunity pays off

After about 3 hours of waiting there is a signal for a good input point. It is at this point that the price reaches the resistance level and the RSI goes to create a divergence. A short position opens for about 30 minutes.

About 3 hours waiting for a good trade signal

After completing your order, forget about it. You did what was in your hands. Now take a breath, relax, take a walk or read a newspaper. Take a break from the markets for about half an hour so you can return with a clear head.

Always remember that patience is the key to success. You can learn it. And don't forget that there are free demo accounts where you can practice trading various assets, strategies and indicators without the risk of losing your money. You can also train your patience.

CHAPTER THREE
THE BEST TOOLS AND SOFTWARE FOR DAY TRADING

Many new traders make the beginner's mistake of using the wrong tools. Important to your success will be finding and using the right day trading software and the right day trading tools. While an experienced trader can settle for instruments that are not exactly ideal, novice traders need every possible advantage.

This means making sure you are equipped with the best trading software, scanning software and charting software.

I often talk about trying to ride a road bike on sand. It doesn't matter if you have a $ 2,000 road bike, you can't ride a road bike on sand.

If you ride a used $ 200 beach bike on fat tires, you're having a blast! The guy on the road bike will wonder why you're making it so easy.

It is because you are using the right equipment for the environment. It's not about how much money you spend, it's about using the right tools. Simplify your life using the best tools below.

Day trading software

There are a few different items you will need for day trading, includi

- Online broker

- Scanning software

- Charting software

- Breaking News Software

Now we are going to analyze which are my favorite day trading software, why to use them and why they are crucial for traders!

Online Broker: Lightspeed Financial Broker

There are hundreds of brokers to choose from and all of them offer traders a different experience.

I generally group brokers into various categories depending on the services they provide or the financial instruments they specialize in. There are options, forex, stocks, long-term investments, and scalping brokers.

There are some things that are important for day traders, such as hotkeys, direct access routing and quick executions.

Because of the above I use Lightspeed and I consider them the best broker and one of the best tools for any trader.

If you trade with a $ 500 trading account, CMEG (Capital Market Elite Group) is your best bet! They allow unlimited daily trading with a balance of $ 500 min (no restrictions of day trader patterns)

Inventory Scanning Software: Trade-Ideas

Now that you have your own funded broker you are ready to start trading! It is useful to have a way to find the actions to trade. Based on my Gap and Go and Momentum trading strategies, there are only a few stocks that are worth trading on any given day.

Knowing how to identify those stocks before they take the plunge is what separates the most profitable traders from everyone else.

Trade-Ideas is great for all my stock scanning software. You can use their predefined searches to see HOD movements, volume peaks, Biggest Gainers/Losers, Turbo Breaks, etc.

Or you can do what I did and build custom scanners using their set of hundreds of filters to tell scanners exactly what you want to see.

Do you like to trade with the Flags of the Bull? No problem. Flat Top Breakouts? Simple. It is the best software in the world able to scan the market and find winning stock settings better than Trade-Ideas.

Graphics Software: eSignal Charting

At this point you have your broker, you are all equipped with Trade-Ideas, and you are ready to get charts of the highest quality. You can safely use the charts that are provided by default by your broker.

These will work for some time, but eventually you may want to level up and use graphs that allow you to draw and write custom formulas.

This is where eSignal comes in. ESignal allows me to easily run graphs on 8 monitors without any delay.

This is pretty impressive. It is important because it allows you to keep an eye on several titles at the same time. Besides being fast and reliable, eSignal allows you to install custom scripts. They are used as custom indicators for reversals and automatically draw support/resistance lines.

Breaking News Provider: Benzinga

Every morning it's good to start the day with a review of the actions gapping up on our Trade-Ideas scans. From there we need to look for the news catalyst, why these headlines move higher. Sometimes they move in sympathy with the market or a strong industry, but other times they have a unique catalyst such as earnings.

It is important to understand why a title moves because some catalysts are stronger than others! We could use Benzinga Pro to search for the latest titles. Then during the day listen to Radio Benzinga Pro.

They read the headlines and inform us when the stocks are up, inform us about the news, etc.

TAS market profile

TAS Market Profile is one of the best day trading software programs out there. There are a couple of different packages that you can choose from depending on what you are looking for.

It also has a suite of TAS indicators that offers 7 of their proprietary indicators including: TAS Market Map, TAS Boxes, TAS Vega, TAS Navigator, TAS Ratio and TAS Compression Levels.

Worth taking into consideration is the TAS Market Map, TAS Vega and TAS Boxes for active and valuable trading decisions.

They also offer TAS Scanner. This unique tool allows you to see actions moving in different periods of time with different levels of buying or selling confidence at key levels. It is a powerful addition to your charting software and is something I use every day.

Indicators and scanners work on many different graphics platforms, including eSignal, Tradestation and Bloomberg.

CHAPTER FOUR
RIGHT STOCKS TO TRADE

Choosing the right stocks to trade
Intraday investment

As can be seen from the name itself, intraday trading (or day trading) presupposes the opening and closing of an operation on the same day, but also a very rapid operation. With this type of trading, the trader never leaves his positions open overnight, because he opens and closes them during the course of the day. To be successful with this strategy, it is therefore important to know how to choose the shares to buy, especially if we consider that the time to think is reduced. Often people are unable to generate profits from intraday trading because they fail to select the proper stocks.

1. Buy only the most liquid shares

Stock liquidity is the most important factor to consider in intraday trading. The more "liquid" shares have huge trading volumes and therefore can be bought and sold in large quantities without significantly affecting the price. Conversely, less liquid ones do not allow traders to buy and sell in large quantities due to the lack of too many buyers. However, some may argue that "illiquid" stocks offer great earning opportunities due to rapid price changes. However, statistics show that volatile stocks show more movement in a short period of time. Thus, most

of the possible gains dissipate while

the downside risk still remains! In any case, the liquidity of the securities depends on the quality of the trades put in place.

2. Stay away from volatile stocks

It is commonly known that a low daily volume of stocks traded or those for which big news are expected always move unpredictably. At times, the stock can show volatility even after the announcement of big news regarding the company in question. This means that day traders should stay away from these types of stocks. Usually, the greatest volatility occurs on small-cap stocks, while mid-cap stocks have a much more linear trend. But in addition to being volatile, these stocks also have low daily trading volumes, which also makes them less liquid.

3. Buy stocks with good correlation

Another way to make intraday trading more profitable is to opt for those stocks that have a higher correlation with major sectors and indices. This means that when the index or sector sees an upward movement, the stock price will rise accordingly. Stocks that move according to the "group sentiment" are always the most reliable and often follow the expected movement of the sector. The strengthening of the Indian rupee against the dollar, for example, will generally affect all information technology companies that depend on the US markets.

4. Follow the trend

One of the most important "tricks" of intraday trading is that following the trend will almost always bring benefits. During a bull market, traders should try to identify those stocks that are potentially bullish. On the other hand, during a bear market, it is advisable to find those stocks that are bound to decline instead.

5. Buy after doing research

Looking for quality companies is one of the pillars of intraday trading. Unfortunately, most day traders today don't do any research before buying. First, you need to identify the benchmark index and then find the sectors that are of interest to you. The next step is to create a list of various stocks belonging to these sectors. Traders don't necessarily need to understand which are the leading companies in the industry, but rather identify the stocks that are more liquid. It is therefore necessary to rely on technical analysis and determine the support and resistance levels together with the study of the fundamentals of these actions, so as to find the most profitable ones for intraday trading.

Medium-long term investment

Day Trading

Actions

Before investing, we need to start from the basics and be aware of what stocks are.

Shares are a financial instrument that allows you to purchase a portion of a company: in fact, they represent a share owned by the company that issues the share.

Ownership of the shares gives the right to participate in the operating and financial results of the company, as well as control of a portion of the company assets.

How the stock market works

The stock market is divided into "Primary Stock Market" and "Secondary Stock Market":

Primary stock market

Newly issued securities are placed in the "Primary Stock Market", here we will find:

New bond issues (such as BOTs or BTPs)

New issues of shares

IPO (initial public offering), i.e. the first public offering of shares belonging to companies that have just been listed on the market

Secondary stock market

The Secondary Stock Market is what interests us most because it is where the trading of shares takes place.

Within the Secondary Market, anyone can buy shares of any company listed on various international markets.

To understand how the stock market works, let's take a trivial example:

I decide to sell 100 Apple shares for $ 200 each.

You think Apple stock is worth more, so you sniff out the deal and buy my 100 shares at $ 200 a share.

The sell and buy orders (which are anonymous) coming from all investors are thus compared, and, since ours are compatible, the trade is made.

What stocks to buy

Now I will give you my personal opinion on which stocks to buy and how to choose the best ones when making an investment with a medium-long time horizon.

First of all I want to give you some positive news: the fundamental characteristic for a successful investment in the stock market is common sense.

In fact, I can assure you that all those mathematical formulas are not necessary for small investors.

Obviously, there are some notions that you need to know, even when deciding on what to bet based mainly on common sense, and below I will explain them one by one.

Behind the shares are the companies

First, remember what you are buying when you buy shares: you are buying shares in a company that you believe is valid.

You will become a full shareholder of the company, albeit at a low percentage of the company's total outstanding shares in the market.

So, if you invest in Amazon stock, you won't be able to sit on Bezos' right on the board of directors, but you will share the fate of his company.

Invest in what you know

If you don't know a business, what's the point of focusing on a company operating in this business?

It pays to invest in sectors and companies that you fully understand.

If you don't know anything about biotechnology, how can you tell if the patents of a company like Bayer are valid compared to those of the competition?

On the other hand, if you are interested in video games, movies or technology and are about to release a new Netflix series or a latest generation Nvidia video card, you could consider buying their shares.

Think about what your skills or passions are and specialize in those fields.

The market looks to the future

The market is forward-looking, i.e. it always looks to the future.

In fact, all official or verified announcements regarding future events will be taken into consideration immediately by the market.

Sometimes this also applies to rumors.

For example, if Apple presents a new innovative iPhone model, the price movements will be immediate and will not wait for the actual release of the smartphone.

Then, when this new product is actually available to the public, the listing will not move in view of the launch of the new device.

In the period of release of the iPhone X (09-2017) the price of Apple shares did not react in a particular way. The significant change occurred in the previous months, - at the beginning of the year.

It is also obvious that if the public were to particularly appreciate the new phone and sales skyrocket, incredibly positive operating results will be reported in the next budget and the price will leap forward again, but the movement will be given by the cash produced, not by the news of the 'iPhone.

So, if you want to invest in a company's project, be careful that this is not already priced by the market, because you may not find the earnings you are looking for until the actual results are published.

Timing of investments

When you invest in the stock market, it is not only important to understand which stocks to bet on, but also when to buy them. In fact, the market is not always efficient in pricing a stock.

It is possible that the market is distracted and underestimating the business potential, resulting in a low share price. It is much more common than you might think.

But, in the long run, the market is supposed to give a fair price to all stocks, it's just a matter of time.

Therefore, the timing of the investment (i.e. the decision of when to open a position) is very important.

Money is sovereign

There is an old saying that is very popular among stock market traders: cash is king.

Money is sovereign: a company that grinds money will most likely be a company to bet on, while a company in constant loss does not seem an attractive investment to me.

An example? Tesla.

For years Tesla has never brought a dollar of profit to its investors, yet the cost of a share has far exceeded $ 700.

This is due to future expectations of what Tesla may become, or, in the opposite view, pure speculation.

There are therefore two types of different companies:

- Valuable companies are those that produce money
- Companies with good growth potential are firms, often relatively young, that record operating losses for a medium to long period of time due to the large investments required to start their business (in fact some fail, so be careful)

What is the attractiveness of companies belonging to this latter category?

If a company with a winning idea but in constant loss starts making money, rest assured it will make a bang.

Best titles: parameters to check

To understand which stocks are the best, my suggestion is to identify stocks of companies with excellent fundamental values, that is, capable of producing large balance sheets and with a fair amount of cash flows.

In other words, focus on the value of companies.

Some of the key indicators of corporate profitability are:

EBITDA: is an important measure of the potential cash flow arising from the company's operating cycle. The higher this number, the better.

PE: is the price/earnings per share ratio and is used to determine the relative value of a company's shares, or if they are expensive. The PE of the action you are interested in should be compared with that of its competitors: for example, in the case within a certain sector the value of the PE is on average around 15, while the PE of the action you observe is 30, the title is considered overrated. If instead the value is 10, it could be a good deal for tomorrow.

EPS: report profits to total outstanding shares. Again, the higher they are, the better.

ROI/ROE: they are simply measures of the return on investment. Again, the higher the value, the better the indicator.

Costs: especially of an operational nature, are obviously viewed negatively by investors. Structured companies that need huge capital and personnel to guarantee their production activities seem to suffer consistently, on financial lists, from the lack of flexibility.

The reading of these values is even more relevant when compared with previous periods.

Furthermore, it is very useful to compare the results of the indicators with those of the competitors of the company in which you are considering investing, so as to have an idea of the company's strength compared to the competition.

However, as reported in Tesla's example, it must be kept in mind that large investors today seem to be heavily focused on business growth. The parameters shown in the list are undoubtedly crucial, but there is the risk, if not supplemented by growth prospects, that they can only provide a partial picture of the goodness of a stock.

Therefore, we pay particular attention to the growth rate, which indicates precisely the annual growth of the company. The measure relies on the ROE and the portion of profits not distributed to shareholders in the form of a dividend, so that it can be reinvested in the company's business lines.

I would like to clarify how the stock market trend is consolidating more and more towards positive evaluations of companies operating in the future and projected towards innovative sectors.

Worst stocks

I would also keep away from all companies that are not able to produce a profit of one euro, especially if consolidated within a business that is not innovative at all and therefore without room for growth.

A fortiori, I would avoid companies that only know how to post losses on their balance sheets.

Conversely, you could use contracts for difference (CFDs) to short sell these companies: short selling is a bit like betting against a company, so that if it goes wrong on the stock market, you can make money.

Unfortunately, I will not name companies that I think are poor (to say the least) because I don't want to be sued.

How to learn to invest in the stock market

There is no magic formula to learn how to operate on the stock market: the only way is to get information, study and experiment.

To learn how to invest in the stock market, start reading finance journals, studying business valuation principles, and using a trading simulator.

Focus primarily on fundamental analysis and pursue stock value.

With fundamental analysis you can be able to evaluate if a company is solid or not, if it is expensive or cheap, if it is profitable for its investors or if it is a slot machine.

Speculation passes, new trends and new fashions will go on the market (Bitcoin, Beyond Meat, etc.), but the value and growth remain.

As far as technical analysis is concerned, some indicators are certainly useful, especially for the timing of an investment (when to enter and when to exit), but I would not decide what to bet on just looking at technical analysis.

I suggest you initially focus on volumes, trend-lines (resistances and supports) and moving averages.

Finally, it is possible to experiment directly on the field thanks to completely free online trading simulators, which allow you to invest in the stock market without putting your capital at risk.

CHAPTER FIVE
STRATEGIS

High-frequency

High Frequency Trading: the secrets of HFT

High Frequency Trading, or HFT, are very high speed trading algorithms, with execution times that are measured in infinitesimal fractions of a second.

What they are and how they operate

Perhaps not everyone knows that, for some years now, those responsible for investment choices - or perhaps it is better to say for trading choices - of the majority of financial giants are no longer (only) men, but also algorithms. The latter have now taken hold so much that in some markets it is estimated that more than half of trading takes place with automatic systems. With peaks that in some cases travel on even much higher percentages.

Algorithmic trading systems delegate to a machine the choice, execution and management of purchase orders. Within algorithmic trading there is a sub-category known by the acronym HFT (High Frequency Trading), which identifies very high-speed trading systems, with execution times that are measured in infinitesimal fractions of a seco

Based on the execution latency and position maintenance, high frequency automatic trading differs significantly from traditional long-term investing and algorithmic trading.

To minimize latency (i.e. the time to send orders) co-location (i.e. proximity to the servers of the exchanges of the machines that send the orders) is essential. So much that in the first months of diffusion of these systems there was a real rush in search of the properties closest to the data processing centers of the stock exchanges around the world, to grab the best locations for the execution of these algorithms.

HFT systems are very popular in the stock market but are also applied to a maximum extent on other assets, such as options, bonds, derivatives and commodities. The duration of the transactions implemented by the HFTs can be very short. The purpose of these algorithms is to profit on very low margins but for a very high number of operations. Only in this way can these systems be profitable. Usually these systems pass a large number of orders to the market (typically in execute immediately or cancel format) but only a very small percentage of them are actually executed. The algorithm then remains in position for a very short time, even a few millionths of a second. At the end of the day, all positions are always closed.

There are numerous techniques used by High Frequency Trading algorithms to operate. Among the most used are:

- arbitrage that exploits discrepancies in the price of a security listed on different stock exchanges also through the analysis of the different degree of liquidity of the markets in question,

- arbitrage between ETFs and its underlying,
- statistical arbitrage, through which correlations between different asset classes are used,
- the exploitation of particular macroeconomic news, through the association of trading strategies with one or more particular keywords present in press releases,
- "order flow detection" techniques, i.e. the identification and exploitation of order blocks,
- "smoking" techniques that plan to entice other operators with proposals then modified at more favorable prices,
- "spoofing" techniques, which involve placing and canceling orders to trick traders into thinking that a certain trend phase has started
- "layering" techniques, with the insertion of a hidden buy order and a clearly visible sell order,
- "pinging" techniques, with the insertion of small purchase proposals to discover the behavior of other traders.

HFT systems have some positive aspects. They usually lower the spreads between bid and ask (i.e. between the best buy and sell proposals), increase the liquidity of an instrument (consequently of a market) and improve the so-called price discovery, i.e. the determination of the price of a financial instrument starting from the information available on that asset. However, they are not exempt from problems, such as the one - of a software nature - which in 2012 caused the collapse (after losses of half a billion dollars) of Knight Capital

or what in May 2012 led to an anomalous trend of the Dow Jones: due to of these high-frequency automatic trading systems, the index, in about ten minutes, went from 10,650 to 9,872 points, before returning to 10,232 points.

It is no coincidence that the supervisory authorities (and in the US even the FBI) have long been committed to monitoring the activities of high-frequency trading algorithms. However, according to staunch critics, the war on HFTs clashes with their ability to create trading volumes. And high turnover means high commissions...

Momentum

Momentum trading is a strategy that uses the force of price movements to open a position, be it long or short. Let's discover some of the main indicators used to trade with this strategy.

Momentum trading is a strategy that takes into account only the price trend to decide whether to buy or sell a particular market. The idea behind the strategy is that if there is a strong enough force behind a certain price movement, then this market will continue to move in the same direction.

When the prices of a market are rising, they often attract the attention of traders and investors, giving an even stronger push to the current movement. This effect lasts until a large number of sellers arrive on the market and find current prices too high. At this point the price rise stops and the market changes direction.

Those who trade with this strategy therefore do not care about the fundamentals of the underlying market or its long-term growth prospects. Rather, traders who take advantage of this strategy try to identify how strong the market trend is before deciding whether to open a position or not.

It should be noted that those who operate with momentum do not necessarily intend to sell on the highs or buy on the lows. Rather it focuses on the central part of the trend, the strongest one, exploiting the market sentiment and the so-called herd effect, or the tendency of operators to follow the 'mass'.

There are three key factors in identifying the Momentum:

Volume

Volatility Time

Time Frame

Volume

Volume represents the amount of an asset traded in a given time frame. Pay attention, the volume does not therefore represent the number of transactions carried out, but the number of units traded - therefore, if three operators buy one security each, it is equivalent to an investor who buys three. The volume in this case is in fact 3 traded securities.

Volume is of vital importance for traders as it allows you to quickly enter and exit positions. A market with a large number of buyers and sellers is called a liquid market, as it is easier to trade an asset. Conversely, a market with a low number of buyers and sellers is considered illiquid and selling or buying the underlying is rather difficult.

Volatility

Volatility is the degree of fluctuation in the price of an asset. If a market is highly volatile, it means that there are large price swings, while a market with low volatility is relatively stable.

If the markets are volatile, traders can take advantage of short- term price rises and falls. It is important to remember to prepare an adequate risk management strategy to protect the operations from adverse market movements by inserting stop losses.

Time frame

Momentum strategies are usually focused on short-term market movements, although the duration of a trade may depend on the strength of the underlying trend. This makes this strategy suitable both for scalpers, i.e. those who operate on time frames ranging from a few seconds to a maximum of one hour, and for investors who have longer investment horizons.

How to start trading momentum

There are several steps to follow to make a strategy of this type. First of all:

- Identify the market of your interest
- Develop a trading strategy based on technical indicators Practice using a risk-free demo account
- Start practicing on live markets

The best momentum indicators

As already mentioned, momentum trading is based solely on the movement of prices. This is why most traders rely primarily on technical analysis and indicators.

In this regard, the most important momentum indicators include:

The momentum

Relative Strength Index (RSI)

Other oscillators, such as Stochastic, CCI, etc.

In general, all oscillators are good momentum indicators. We specify that oscillators fall within a particular category of indicators that analyze situations of overbought (excess demand) or oversold (excess supply).

Momentum

As the name implies, it is undoubtedly the most important indicator for this strategy. The operation is extremely simple: it takes the most recent closing price and compares it with the closing price of n previous periods. Obviously, the choice of the number of previous periods is arbitrary, even if usually on trading platforms there are often default values of 10, 12 or 14.

The oscillator is made up of a single line that moves around the center line of zero. The value of the indicator line gives traders an idea of the strength of the underlying trend. Obviously it will take on a positive value when the difference between the last close and that of n previous candles is positive. If the indicator line crosses the zero line from the bottom, then it means that the price is rising and has exceeded the closing levels of n periods ago. It could therefore be a potentially bullish sign. Conversely, if the indicator crosses zero from above, the sales are strengthening and the signal is potentially bearish.

Although some traders use the indicator to enter and exit positions, most traders use it to confirm if there is a trend in place.

Relative Strength Index (RSI)

The Relative Strength Index (RSI) is an indicator that moves from 0 to 100 and provides overbought and oversold signals depending on its value. If it rises above 70 the market is overbought, while if it falls below 30 it is oversold. Like the Momentum indicator, it is plotted on a separate chart and falls under the oscillators.

When using the RSI, it is important to note the overbought and oversold signal does not necessarily mean that the trend will change. It could also represent a simple pause in the current trend, before it regains strength.

Sometimes this indicator is also used to see if there are any divergences in the market, i.e. phases in which prices rise to

new highs (fall to new lows) while the RSI does not reach the previous highs (lows).

Summary

Momentum trading is the strategy that allows you to buy and sell an asset based on the recent price trend.

Traders will open a position to take advantage of a strengthening trend and close the position when it starts to lose strength.

Momentum trading is based on volume, volatility and time frame.

The strategy does not involve studies on long-term fundamental or growth, rather it looks at short-term price action.

The best known indicators for momentum trading are the Momentum oscillators, the RSI and the Stochastic.

Pre-market and after-market

Not everyone knows that it is possible to carry out stock trading activities even outside the normal market session.

The period in which you can execute operations on the stock market before the opening of continuous trading is called pre- market, while the corresponding time frame after closing is called after-market.

The times of these two intervals depend on the exchange on which we wish to operate and on the conditions defined by the broker we have chosen to carry out our financial transactions.

If we intend to operate in these sessions, it is useful first to carefully evaluate the constraints imposed by the financial intermediary, so that we can plan our operations without surprises.

Although the methods of entering orders are the same as on the daytime exchange, market conditions are different and exchanges, in the pre-market and after-market, present both undoubted advantages and risks.

The main advantage of operating outside the institutional market is the fact that companies almost always disclose their economic results, such as earnings data, before or after the close of trading, so many operators are interested in seizing the opportunity to intervene immediately on the news.

It should be emphasized that this type of operation requires a lot of speed and coldness, so it is not suitable for everyone, but if you can follow the right direction you can get great satisfaction.

Another advantage is represented by the fact of being able to observe the performance of a stock during the pre-market and therefore, make an operational decision when the market opens, when volumes increase quickly.

In the face of these earnings opportunities, there are of course risks to be taken into consideration which, in the pre-market and in the after-market, have particular characteristics.

The first risk to consider is the lack of liquidity:

In fact, for many shares, in these two market sessions, the trading volumes are much lower than the regular trading hours, this can make it more difficult to complete our operation.

Higher spreads:

The scarcity of volumes can result in a larger difference between bid and ask, so order execution will be more difficult or you may risk getting a less advantageous price.

Possible increase in volatility:

In this context, higher price fluctuations may be encountered than in continuous trading. This situation could also be an advantage, but you need to be able to manage sudden movements in prices.

During the pre and after-market, you have to deal with many professionals from large institutions.

They operate a lot during these hours and, as we know, they have access to much more information than small traders, also having a very high technological power.

In conclusion, the activities before and after the opening of continuous quotations represent excellent earning opportunities, but it is necessary to carefully study this type of market before operating as it presents some pitfalls that should not be underestimated.

CHAPTER SIX

SUCCESSFUL TRADE
How to create an efficient trading plan

What is a trading plan?

A trading plan is a project or a set of guidelines that helps you outline your trading activity. This tool can be particularly useful for planning and implementing a negotiation strategy.

There is no absolute model to follow to get a perfect trading plan (each trader is unique and different styles suit different people), but there are universally accepted elements to be taken into consideration when drawing up a personal plan.

The trading plan can also be compared to a business plan. You would never start a business without a valid project: why starting a commercial activity without a trading plan?

General rules of the trading plan

Even if it is true that there is no absolute model to refer to in order to draw up a perfect trading plan, there are still some general rules that can help you in most cases.

1. Put it in writing. You should physically write down (or type in) your reasons for trading and the main goals you hope to achieve.
2. This will help you to organize your thoughts, and solidify your

plan.

2 Record your progress. Develop a clear and concise method for recording your trading activities.

When planning a long-term strategy it is essential to be able to see past and present investments, both from a learning perspective and keeping track of the markets you trade in or are exposed to.

3 Check your financial situation. Capital management is another crucial element of the trading plan. You need a plan to manage your investments, especially your risk exposure.

Main questions about trading plan

Here are some important questions to consider when drafting your trading plan:

What is your motivation for trading? What is your risk appetite?

How much time can you dedicate to trading? What is your level of knowledge?

When creating a trading plan, the answers to these questions must be taken into account. Only by knowing our goals and capabilities will we be able to build the trading plan that best suits our characteristics.

Why using a trading plan? Here are all the benefits

The trading plan can be a valuable aid in many situations:

A. Configure facilities to better manage risk

What does the term high or low risk mean to you? By quantifying it in advance, you can apply a scientific approach to assess whether a particular trade is too risky. Your risk scale for the size of the trade could be as follows:

Low risk: 1-2% of the total fee Medium risk: 2-5% of the total share

High risk: More than 5% of the total share

Highly reckless: Over 20% of the total share

For example: With an account of $ 10,000, a 3% risk equals $ 300 on a single transaction (average risk).

Another way to consider risk is to set a risk/reward ratio. The risk is represented by the loss of a trade or when the market takes the stop loss, the return is instead the gain of an transaction or when the market moves in the direction favorable to us and reaches the target. Usually in an efficient trading plan the risk/reward ratio is equal to 1/2 or 1 / 3. Risk 1 to earn 2. Risk 1 to earn 3. In these cases, even with a 50% probability of success of my trading strategies will still have a positive balance.

B. Establish entry and exit strategies in advance

In many, if not most cases, being able to optimize your income and expenses is the most stressful part of the whole transaction.

Nowadays, there is often the risk of basing a decision on an emotional response rather than a strategic one. For this reason, it can be extremely useful to establish clear criteria and rules to be followed for the management of income and expenditure.

For example, you can use charts to monitor market trends and decide to initiate a trade only when particular patterns emerge. Alternatively, when considering closing a position, you can set profit/loss limits to adhere to as the position evolves.

It can be very helpful to have a set of guidelines established by you in a rational environment, away from the pressure of an ongoing transaction.

c.Stay focused and optimize decision making

Financial markets can move very quickly and it is at these times that you may feel overwhelmed and more prone to making hasty decisions.

A trading plan is a vital reference point in these situations, as many decisions are made in advance, before being faced with inevitable problems. Act on your plan rather than making decisions on the spot.

A trading plan can help keep the excitement out of trading. Some people may attribute profits to emotions or instinct, but long-term success will almost always be based on a carefully thought out and worked out strategy in advance.

D. Continuously evaluate transactions and manage money

A trading plan often includes a trading ledger or diary, which you can use to track all executed trades and make a note of their success or failure.

A trading log is an excellent tool that allows you to have a clear view of the big picture. In one image you can encapsulate your trading history and identify the successes and mistakes made along the way.

Honesty and self-awareness are important traits, but constant trading evaluation is one of the best ways to avoid repeating mistakes and to remember things that worked in the past.

E. Simplify trading and maintain discipline

A trading strategy can continually remind you of the goals you have achieved and the limits you have set for yourself.

A written plan is very useful for maintaining your trading discipline - it is increasingly difficult to deviate from the original plan when you always have it in front of your eyes. Keep it on your desk or hang it on the wall if needed.

Who needs a trading plan?

The synthetic answer to this question is: everyone. From newbies to professionals, no one can say they can really do without a trading plan.

Your experience will undoubtedly influence the extent to which you use and benefit from a trading plan, but using a trading plan according to your needs is undoubtedly in your best interest.

You decide how to use the trading plan, but in the next section we have highlighted some essential tips on how to create it. You can also see examples of a trading plan and log.

How to make a trading plan?

The 9 basic steps to build your trading plan is a tool that you shape by adapting it to your personal trading style. You are free to include any items you find useful in the plan, but by following these steps you will be sure that you have included all the essentials.

1. Know your trader skills

First of all, you need to complete the following sentence: 'I want to be a successful trader because...'

Secondly, you need to honestly assess your strengths and weaknesses, not only with regard to trading, but also with respect to any personal traits that may affect the way you trade.

2. Define and understand your trading goals

Defining trading goals is one of the most important steps in developing a trading plan. It is also the stage that many people overlook.

You must try to be very precise and scrupulous in terms of both profit and timing. Only by defining and quantifying your goals will you be able to assess the extent to which you have achieved them.

Many trading plans suggest that you identify your goals on a daily, weekly, monthly, semi-annual, yearly, or lifetime basis.

It may seem silly or impossible to set daily trading goals or set a goal to be pursued over a lifetime. But, more than the actual result, it is the thinking behind these goals that is important and beneficial.

3. Decide which types of trading you are interested in

You have several trading options on the financial markets. Some people prefer to stick to one method, others have successfully integrated different types of trading into the same plan.

Whatever path you decide to take, it is essential that you understand the options available to you and make the decision, as part of your trading plan, to stick to a particular system.

Of course, you can change your trading plan as your trader skills increase, but what you should avoid is trying a new type of trading on a whim, without trying to figure out if it suits your trading style. Only change your trading plan when you are almost certain that it will be more efficient for your trading.

4. Identify your markets and trading times

Besides knowing what types of trading you are interested in, you should also identify the markets that are best for you.

A first consideration is your level of preparation on particular markets (stocks, commodities, indices, foreign currencies) and the factors that drive them. The more you know, and the more interested you are in the subject, the more you will pay attention.

Likewise, you should consider the opening hours of these markets and evaluate your ability to offer them adequate attention during trading hours.

5. Establish your personal trading system

A trading system will apply a set of rules to turn trading into an automated process. You will have to decide if you prefer automatic (or algorithmic) trading where you choose a trading system and let this guide all your decisions, or discretionary, where you make decisions on a case-by-case basis.

6. Know how much you are willing to risk

Risk management is the most important aspect of a trading plan. There are many techniques for managing risk, from position sizing strategies to risk minimization tactics.

From the perspective of the trading plan it is important to consider money management, in order to adapt to your trading style and stick to it regardless of the trading conditions.

The following questions should be asked:

What percentage of my account am I ready to risk in each trade?

How many positions am I ready to manage at the same time?

What is the maximum exposure of the account that I am ready to accept?

How much risk do I want to take for each position?

7. Decide how you want to manage your open positions

This aspect of the trading plan concerns the management of open positions. This is the situation where you are most exposed to emotional reactions - you see the market go down and you want to reduce your losses, or the market is frozen and you are tempted to hold the position even longer.

In these emotionally charged situations it is essential to already have a strategy to appeal to. The advice is always to trust your trading plan strategies. Only by being disciplined will you see results in the long run.

8. Plan to store your trading data

It is surprising how often people overlook this aspect of the trading plan, especially considering that it can be a very valuable learning tool. Regularly updating the document containing all of your previous transactions, including the details that made them successful or not, can be a valuable lesson for the future. Having a trading agenda is essential.

A simple spreadsheet is the only record you need to keep, but a comments section is very useful. Include everything from the ease with which you followed your strategy, and what worked and what didn't, to what you felt on a given day or hour.

You will be pleasantly surprised at how simple it is to identify successful trends and repeat them in the future.

9. Test your system

You can test the system of your choice by comparing it with historical data to determine if it would hold up to recent market movements. You can do this manually or choose one of the many systems provided by certain financial service providers.

Set your personal goals

What are the factors to consider before investing? The purposes of your trading must be clear and above all they must show us the amount of time we intend to dedicate to our investment.

Time and performance are the two key factors when it comes to understanding your goals and evaluating how to act. Without having carefully weighed what you want to achieve, it will be difficult to obtain good returns.

Imagine you have a garden to take care of, which you want to see grow over time. You don't know what will happen tomorrow, in a few months or in a few years, but your goal is to make it a well-kept garden in every respect.

The garden metaphor is one of the most used to explain how an investment works, what its variables are, what it depends on, and what its main goals are.

Here are some tips to understand how to calculate your investment goals and how to avoid mistakes.

Trading Goals: Time and Return

The two key factors determining the investment are time and yield.

These two elements, of course, are proportional. The performance, in fact, depends on the time we have chosen.

First of all, consider the timing, since you will have to choose the right tool based on it. Investing in CFDs has different timing than investing in mutual funds.

Space-time is therefore the first factor to be calculated as a preliminary element.

We will then move on to understand what is the return you want to achieve, in order to have a clear trading strategy. The return you want to get from your investment must also be related to the timing.

Trading goals: short, medium and long term investments

First of all, investments are divided into three different typologies: there are short-term investments, medium-term investments and long-term investments.

For short-term investments we mean an investment load not exceeding 12/18 months and are usually adopted to invest a certain part of liquidity that can be available in the short term.

The ideal financial instruments for short-term investments are represented by Bots, 12/18 month CCTs, 12/18 month BTPs, AAA government bonds belonging to the Eurozone in order to avoid exchange rate risks.

Short-term investing is also an ideal tactical solution for weighing other investment strategies.

On the other hand, as regards medium/long-term investments, it is necessary to pay due attention to all financial instruments and to have in-depth knowledge on the subject, especially for long-term investments. In fact, it is highly advisable to get the assistance of a professional in the sector.

Medium/long-term investments are useful for achieving certain objectives, such as increasing one's capital, maintaining purchasing power unchanged over time, protecting it from real inflation, or guaranteeing a substantial income for a supplementary pension.

Investment objectives: here are the main ones

The main objectives of the investment include the following:

- Accumulation, if you want to invest to increase your assets to be bequeathed to our years;

- Decumulus, to be connected with the pension position, which however allows us to constantly maintain our standard of living;

- Flow objectives, to obtain a periodic income starting from a certain time, in order to maintain a constant standard of living, even in difficult times ;

- Capital objectives, to increase your capital over time, aimed for example at planning large expenses in the future.

Everyone has its own precise purposes, but usually these are the goals that are taken into consideration the most and which are adopted to design their trading strategy.

Trading objectives: expected return

- The expected return represents the relationship between the expected result and the invested capital. The expected return can be listed in the following types:

- Physiological return: aimed at safeguarding purchasing power, commensurate with the expected inflation rate;

- Minimum return: usually obtained with short- term government bonds, generally at zero risk;

- Return higher than the free risk rate: determined by a higher level of risk, the return is higher but in comparison with an equally higher level of risk.

Trading objectives: some useful advice

No joking with the investment, it is necessary to have in-depth knowledge of the subject or to have acquired some experience, or even be supported by a professional.

Here are some tips to follow:

- Identify your needs;
- Do not make hasty judgments and always consider the predetermined time factor;

- Understand if you are more inclined to a greater risk appetite or if you are more prudent;

- Constantly maintain a relationship with your consultant based on clarity and transparency.

How does intraday trading differ from classic trading?

One of the main differences between intraday trading and regular trading is time. In intraday, the trader is required to close the position the same day before the market closes, regardless of the profit or loss. In classic trading, the trader can choose to keep the position open for even longer than one day and in any case there is no time limit for closing the operation.

Come in and out at the right time

A great idea is to trade following an intraday trend. This offers the potential for low-risk entry points, while providing high earning potential if the trend continues. To identify these patterns, I invite you to read the related article "How to exploit market trends with a trading strategy with the stochastic".

To identify when to quit, two conditions can be observed; the first is when you have reached the target, the second is when you have reached the maximum loss limit below which you do not want to go (stop loss).

Always have a stop loss level set

Having a stop loss set is one of the basic rules of intraday trading. The stop loss is the exit level and the tool for capital protection in case your trend or expectations do not come true. On the other hand, if the predictions are correct, you should have set different price targets in which to profit from the trade.

The historical returns factor

We all believe that "history repeats itself". While this cannot be said with 100% certainty, financial markets usually follow their own historical path as well. Therefore, the goal should be to find a strategy that preserves capital and at the same time offers returns at a controlled risk.

You can choose to start trading after analyzing the trend of a specific asset and understanding its characteristics. Also, remember to choose the liquid asset that has a high average daily volume which will guarantee numerous opportunities.

Don't be impulsive

Traders often feel discouraged if their trading strategy doesn't work as hoped. Beginners should use historical analysis to find opportunities and build simple trading strategies.

A trader, before entering the market, should have a well- defined level of profit and stop loss and should not let impulsive nature take control of the trading activity. If you've devised an entry-and-exit strategy that best aligns with your needs, don't change it impulsively. Successful trading requires a strong ability to control personal emotions.

Start small

Some good exchanges could boost your confidence, and if that happens, don't get carried away by your strong ego. Don't be aggressive with your trades early on, focus on up to 1-2 assets to get started. Over time, the volume and size of the operation should increase.

Start small will allow you to make smaller mistakes and increase your familiarity with how the market works so you don't make the same mistakes twice. Gradually increase the trading volume as your experience and risk appetite increases.

Keep calm

Since intraday trading requires you to be hyper-vigilant about the market, it certainly brings anxiety with it. However, don't let emotions get the better of you. Decisions should be based on logic and a set strategy. Emotions such as fear, greed, etc. they should be kept at bay.

Alternatives to intraday trading

As mentioned above, intraday trading is very profitable but carries a high degree of risk.

The most common alternative to intraday trading is Swing trading. Swing trading is the trading technique that allows you to open a position on a certain market, short or long, and close it in a few days, capturing the sentiment that governs the trend of prices and the consequent expected price fluctuation.

This investment method is halfway between intraday trading and buy and hold: in a nutshell, swing trading means taking a position in line with the main trend of the underlying, keeping it for a few days.

Risk management

Money Management, Risk Management, Position Sizing, Bet Sizing... no matter what you call it, the important thing is to know it!

When you lose money, you find yourself with less capital to work with and to recover the loss you need to achieve a much higher percentage performance than the one you just lost.

Losing money is in fact negative in itself, but even worse is losing so much money that it definitively jeopardizes the chances of continuing as an investor. It is therefore of fundamental importance to adopt constant behavior by adopting capital protection techniques, which must in no way be disregarded.

Over the last few years there has been a proliferation of people who tried to invest their money independently, without consulting professionals, often using the online trading services offered by any banking institution or broker.

Few traders and managers, however, have developed the necessary disciplinary skills and have a clear understanding of money management strategies.

During the "speculative bubble" talking about strategies to limit risk was practically useless as all the markets were rising dramatically. In recent years, however, due to the well-known movements that are not always easily predictable (price actions), the importance of money management and risk management techniques has once again been realized.

Money Management, in simple terms, tells you how many contracts (or shares, or assets) you can work on at a certain time considering certain portfolio and risk parameters.

It is practically impossible to earn money without the correct use of Money Management techniques.

Money Management is a defensive concept; it allows you to stay on the market in a way that you won't be excluded from it. For example, it tells you if you have enough new money to invest in new positions. Money management should not be confused with the stop loss.

Statistics confirm that 90% of traders lose money, 5% reach break-even and only 5% manage to make money. Often, the losing trader could be part of that 10% that at least reaches break-even if only he were able to correctly size his trades.

Money management is risk management

Proper risk management is the difference between winning and losing trading. Operating correctly on the market is 90%made up of money and portfolio management; this is a fact that most people cannot or do not want to understand.

Once you have the correct Money Management, discipline and psychology complete the figure of the good investor.

Money Management serves to optimize the use of capital

Few people manage to see their wallet as a whole. Even fewer investors/managers are able to take the step from a defensive or reactive view of risk (in which they measure the risk to avoid losses: the risk suffered, i.e. the stop loss.) Towards an aggressive and proactive view in which the risks are actively managed for a more efficient use of capital.

Money management "basic guide"

It must be clear to those who are about to operate on the markets that the fundamental point to keep in mind is the protection and safeguarding of their capital. Only if you manage not to decrease the efficiency of your capital can you hope to stay on the market long enough to be able to continue operating. If you are convinced of this, if you consider it much more important than desperately looking for a gain, caught in the frenzy that is very similar to the one that assails the gamblers, then you are on the right track .

First of all, pay close attention to the drawdown, understood as "the amount of money that can be lost in trading, expressed in terms of percentage of the total available capital" (drawdown is the difference between a peak and a valley in an equity line graph).

The trading system or operating technique that you intend to adopt, or that you have used up to now, must have a maximum drawdown that does not affect the efficiency of your capital. Let's look at some guiding elements.

Tips for simple risk management

- risk a percentage of 2% of the available capital for each operation;

- avoid the use of "financial leverage" (or at least ensure that the borrowed capital does not represent a high percentage of your cash availability);

- invest a maximum of 20% of the capital present in the portfolio;

- for every dollar risked, propose to earn two or three. For example, if you trade with $ 5,000, setting a stop loss at 3% ($ 150 risk) the target should be at least $ 300 / $ 450. In other words, the risk/reward ratio must be at least 1: 2 or better 1: 3;

- before opening a position, always evaluate the volatility of the market (on which it is also possible to calibrate the stop loss);

- monetize at least part of the profits made;

- the higher the operation, the lower the risk level must be; never increase or mediate a losing position;

- if you do not have the technique, avoid pyramiding (increase of the investment in a winning position);

- do not proceed with "mental" stops, but with sell orders actually placed.

A recommendation above all: when you run into a consecutive series of losing operations, it is better to stop the activity and re-evaluate your operating methodology. The legendary William D. Gann wrote, over fifty years ago:

Money management can be applied using a variety of techniques and strategies. From the simplest, linked to "common sense" to the more complex ones consisting of the application of mathematical models.

For most traders it may be sufficient to apply the rules of "common sense" to be able to survive for a long time and profitably to their trading system and the market.

The main rules for proper risk management

<u>Don't be under-capitalized</u>

It is important to have adequate capital for the instrument (future or equity) on which we are going to operate and not to take excessive risks. These two principles help you survive long enough to be able to thrive. There are numerous examples of traders with small capital that were quickly "eliminated" at the beginning of their career.

This concept can be exposed by analyzing a mechanical trading system (Trading System). Let's assume the system has an all-time high drawdown (for example over 5 years) of $ 10,000. Open a trading account with $ 10,000 that is the maximum drawdown and start trading following the signals that the Trading System produces. Let's assume that after a short time you begin to suffer a series of consecutive stop- losses that bring you $ 2,000 in your account. Now its efficiency has greatly diminished and even if the system starts producing good signals again, your portfolio is no longer in a position to work to follow them. Let's say you reset the initial $ 10,000 at this point and the system runs into a maximum drawdown. You are out of the game.

Your "failure" does not depend on the Trading System you were using, but depends exclusively on not having been adequately capitalized to follow the signals that your system generates in the long term.

You and your trading account should be prepared for a drawdown of at least double what a back-testing of your Trading System tells you (and for profits, take into account half of those indicated by back-testing). In the above example, if the all-time high drawdown was $ 10,000, you should have a starting account of at least 20,000 or more.

Risk, in a single transaction, should represent only a small percentage of the available capital, preferably no more than 2% of your portfolio.

You can build up fortunes in the long run even by trading only 2-3 contracts at a time.

The important thing is to survive long enough to continue working on the market, without being "wiped out"

Use real stop orders

Enter them immediately after taking a position on the market. "Mental" stop-losses don't work! Keep the maximum drawdown low (20-25%).

Limit the risk of your entire portfolio to a maximum of 20%

In other words, if you were to suffer stop-loss at the same time in all the positions you had taken, make sure that 80% of the starting capital still remains.

Maintain a reward/risk ratio (= return/risk) at a minimum of 2:1 and preferably 3:1 or more

If you risk 1 point try to have a target of at least 2, better 3 points.

Be realistic about the actual risks required to participate in the market for a certain instrument

For example, do not underestimate the risk of an overnight position in a very volatile security or on a leveraged instrument such as in the Standard & Poor's futures market ($ 250 per point for the main contract, $ 50 per point for the minimum).

Study the volatility of the market on which you are about to operate and adjust the size of the position (position sizing) to the conditions of the volatility itself

Take smaller positions in highly volatile markets. Be aware that volatility is cyclical.

Understand the correlation between different markets and your positions

If you are "long" on heating oil, crude oil and gas, you don't actually have 3 different positions! This is because these markets are highly correlated, you actually have a position in the energy sector with three times the risk of just one position. It would be the same as having three positions in crude oil, or three in heating oil.

Never add positions to positions that are at a loss (average down)

If you find yourself on the wrong side, against the market, admit it quickly and close the position. Your ego is often detrimental to proper trading.

Try to block at least part of the profits you are making

If you are lucky enough to take a substantial move in a short time, liquidate at least part of the position. This rule is especially valid for short-term trading where large gains are few.

The more active you are, the more trades you make and the lower the risks for each trade should be

If you make dozens of trades a day you can't afford to risk 3% on each trade - a bad day could "blow you away" (if, for example, you suffer 10-15 stop-losses in a row your capital would lose efficiency). Long-term traders, those who make 5-7 trades per year, can risk more on each trade (say 3-5% per trade). Regardless of how active you are in the market, however, limit your portfolio risk to 20%.

Apply the pyramiding technique correctly

Only add positions to profitable positions and make sure that the largest position is that of the first trade. For example, if you normally take portfolio positions of 1000 shares per stock, make sure you buy 600 with the first trade. Then add 300 (if the first trade becomes profitable) and finally another 100 if the stock moves further in the direction you want. Moreover, if you pyramide, be sure that the total risk of the position follows the rules previously indicated (for example, 2% in the whole operation, total portfolio risk not exceeding 20%, etc.)

Take advantage of the position when it is in your favor

Once the profit you are making in the operation has exceeded the figure that corresponded to your initial risk, close a part of the position and bring the stop-loss to the value of the breakeven.

Get to know the market you are operating in

This rule is especially valid in the derivatives market (options, futures).

When you have suffered a series of consecutive losses, stop and re-evaluate the market and your working methodology

The market will always be there waiting for you. Gann summarizes the concept in his book "How to make profits in commodities", published more than 50 years ago:

Consider the psychological impact of losing money

Contrary to many other rules discussed here, the psychological impact is difficult to quantify. Each individual reacts differently. You have to ask yourself honestly, "What could happen if I lose xxx $? Would it have a material impact on my lifestyle? And what about my family or my psychological state? You should learn to accept the consequences of suffering a series of consecutive stop-losses. Emotionally, you should be fully aware of the risks you are taking.

Avoid making "hope" your strategy

The main point is to understand that money management practically consists in understanding that it is necessary to study the risk that the investment entails in order to be able to risk only a small percentage on each operation, keeping the total exposure within reasonable margins. The above list is not completely exhaustive, but it should help avoid most problems.

Those who survive long enough on the markets to become successful traders are not just students of trading methodologies and disciplined applicants of such methodologies; they are also students of the risks associated with their techniques.

Glossary of survival and rules of operation

1. Do not commit more than 10% of the capital in a single trade
2. Do not have more than 5 trading operations open at the same time (= max 50% on the capital)
3. Always use an appropriate stop loss and do not move or remove it once placed
4. Identify a goal, both for each individual operation and for all your trading activity
5. If the trend turns out to be favorable, insert and adjust a stop profit level
6. Let profits run and cut losses
7. Do not allow a profit to turn into a loss
8. Do not open a trade if it conflicts with the trend
9. If in doubt it is better to close and, if in doubt, it is better not to open
10. Never mediate a losing trade: wait or close
11. Regarding the cyclicality of the markets: looking for opportunities in both directions
12. Establish risk/return ratios for trading operations of at least 2: 1
13. After a loss do not increase the percentage, but decrease it until you have recovered
14. Pyramiding only on very clear and very strong trends
15. Trade only on liquid markets/securities

16. Do not operate on options, warrants or derivatives if you do not fully understand the mechanisms and risks

17. Do not buy or sell just because the price is low or high

18. Never follow the advice of the "well informed", especially relatives, friends or bank tellers

Rules of conduct

1. Always follow the rules of operation

2. Be disciplined, disciplined and still disciplined

3. Think autonomously, independently and stick to your guidelines. Do not follow the crowd!

4. Understanding and mastering emotions, especially uncertainty, fear and greed

5. Keep it simple: complexity breeds confusion

6. Remain humble: too much confidence lead to the worst losses

7. Be patient: knowing how to wait for the right opportunities is one of the trader's greatest skills

8. Have the strength to admit a mistake and close even if at a loss

9. Do not operate if you are not calm and physically fit

10. Do the analysis and/or study your own closed market strategies

11. Maintain a perspective - also in terms of operating weight - between short, medium and long trends

12. Be objective: having the courage to face the reality of the market

13. Have the strength to maintain a position or a strategy against everything and everyone

14. Be flexible and ready to change strategy quickly if the technical situation changes

15. Do not close out of impatience, but above all do not open out of anxiety about losing an opportunity

16. Diversify in terms of both markets and stocks

17. Refrain from trading after large gains or large losses

18. Remember that the market is a machine for disappointing, but it is always right

Trading indicators

Beginner traders can use some trading indicators, available for free, which help to improve immediately the performance obtained on the financial markets with trading activity. The proposed indicators are very simple to use and therefore are particularly suitable even for beginners.

How are the best indicators for trading made? Here are some key features of the best indicators:

Works well

It is easy to use

It is free

They work well

The first point on our list is truly the most important. In fact, having a trading indicator that is free, easy to use and makes you lose money is certainly not advisable.

What does it mean that a trading indicator works? It means that it is possible to obtain good results when trading online by following the indications of the indicator.

In short, the best indicators simply tell us whether we should trade up or down and the prediction comes true in most cases. No trading indicator is able to correctly predict the market in 100% of the cases: it is mathematically impossible. However, the best indicators manage to provide accurate predictions almost always.

They are easy

Doing complicated mathematical calculations to get the indicator, perhaps without even the support of a software, is a real madness. Usually you are wrong, especially if you have little experience. A complex trading indicator to use is never good, not even for the most experienced and seasoned wolf of the markets, let alone for a beginner.

The best trading indicators are therefore very simple to use: the perfect indicator for a beginner should automatically provide the suggestion to go up or down.

They are free

Spending a fortune to pay for a subscription to trading indicators services is not very convenient, especially if the trading volumes are not high. In short, if I start trading online with a capital of $ 100, it makes no sense to pay $ 1000 a month for a professional trading indicators service. If, on the other hand, I have a millionaire capital, then yes, I can afford to invest more. However, novice traders usually start with $ 100 or $ 200, certainly not millions.

1. MACD (Moving Average Convergence Divergence)

The MACD indicator is one of the most used in the field of technical analysis. It is considered by industry insiders as an essential resource due to the fact that it can provide a truly impressive amount of market data.

The MACD consists of a series of elements that interact with each other and each one is able to generate trading signals. In particular, when using this indicator it is necessary to pay attention to the movements of the so-called MACD line and the Signal Line. The intersection between these two lines can offer trading signals.

A further element to consider is the MACD histogram which is able to show the market volumes, a very important factor that speaks about how much participation there is on a given asset at a certain time.

2 – Simple Moving Average

Known in English as the "Simple Moving Average", the moving average is the basic indicator of all trading activity both online and offline. Anyone involved in financial markets cannot fail to know the moving average and all the potential it can express during the investment phase.

The moving average represents an "average" of the price. Once calculated on the basis of data entered directly by the trader, it is expressed through a function that is displayed directly on the price chart.

The Moving Average is a trading indicator, which means that it is used by traders in order to identify the current trend, trying to understand its changes. It can be used alone or accompanied by other moving averages calculated differently.

3 - Pivot Point Indicator

A very special trading indicator are the so-called Pivot Points, with French pronunciation. The indicator in question is used because it serves to find the so-called "key points of the market". These are particular price areas that are always held in high consideration by the market.

Around the Pivot Points the market tends to behave as if it is in proximity to supports and resistances (another fundamental indicator in the field of online trading). For this reason, the study and use of Pivot Points can provide generally very interesting and reliable trading signals for traders who are able to grasp capture them.

4 - Supports and Resistors

Other indicators that you really cannot do without in the negotiation phase are the supports and resistances. They represent actually a graphic indicator, consequently the trader has to draw the supports and resistances on the price chart himself in order to take them into account and predict the next market developments.

Supports and resistances are limit areas of the price that the market cannot overcome respectively on the downside or the upside. Based on the strength and duration of a support or resistance, it is also possible to determine the reliability of the trading signals generated by the break of one of these price levels.

Plotting supports and resistances is simple: just note which are certain price quotas that have not been exceeded increasing or decreasing after several attempts by the market. There it will be necessary to trace some half-lines that indicate the pivotal point to be examined.

5 - Trend Lines

Very similar to supports and resistances are the trend lines. In any trading activity, it is essential to identify the current market trend. In other words, a trader must understand if the price is in a bullish or bearish phase of the price and act accordingly.

Thanks to the trend lines it is possible to immediately identify which phase the market is in, but also to understand if there are signs of a trend reversal or if the trend is still stable.

Each trend is made up of a succession of highs and lows that increase or decrease depending on the case. When this condition does not exist, we can speak of a market in lateral phase or not in trend. The breakdown of these dynamic supports and resistances marks a good time to enter the market.

6 - RSI oscillator

As you have understood now that we have talked about indicators of all kinds, in the analysis phase it is always important to identify the limit areas of the market. If there is an indicator capable of doing this, it is the RSI oscillator.

The RSI is precisely an oscillator, this means that it will not be displayed directly on the price chart, but below it because here its oscillation between the values of zero and 100 is configured. Based on where the RSI will be, it will be possible to understand the market phase.

In particular, the RSI is useful for identifying the overbought and oversold phases. We are talking about market excesses where buyers or sellers have prevailed for too long and too strongly. The RSI is able to show a similar situation by swinging between the above values.

Recognizing when a market is overbought or oversold is crucial because it helps to understand what the next wisest move to take in market trading will be.

7 - Bollinger bands

Another fundamental indicator for online trading are the so- called Bollinger Bands, an indicator named after their discoverer and inventor John Bollinger. These are a trend indicator that is based just on the simple moving average like many other trading indicators.

The bands get their name from the fact that they are 3 curves that move along with the price and constantly wrap around it. The crucial phases in the observation of this indicator come when we observe the price approaching the upper or lower band, here the trading signals are generated.

8 ADX

The ADX is also a trend indicator and is used to measure the strength of the trend. It was invented by Welles Wilder to obtain information on the trends of commodities, but is now permanently used for the analysis of other markets such as Forex where it has also proved to be very effective.

The indicator is made up of two variables + DI and - DI. By observing these elements it is possible to understand the strength of the current trend and its direction both in a bullish and bearish sense. With these data in hand, the trader is able to understand if it is convenient for him to invest up or down and make the purchase of the correct market position.

CHAPTER SEVEN

10 MISTAKES TO AVOID

Making mistakes is part of the learning process when it comes to trading. Traders generally buy and sell stocks more frequently and hold positions for much shorter periods than traditional investors. This frequent trading and shorter holding periods can lead to mistakes that could quickly wipe out a new trader's invested capital.

While traders of all ages are guilty of the following mistakes from time to time, the novice trader should be especially careful not to make these types of mistakes.

1. No trading plan

Experienced traders enter trading with a well-defined plan. They know their exact entry and exit points, the amount of capital to invest in the trade, and the maximum loss they are willing to take. Beginner traders may not have a trading plan in place before starting trading; and even if they have a plan, they may be more inclined to abandon it than experienced traders would be if things were not going well. Or they may reverse course altogether, for example, going short after buying a stock initially because its price is falling, only to end up getting whipsawed.

Pursuing performance against rebalancing

Many investors choose asset classes, strategies, managers and funds based on recent strong performance. The feeling that "I'm missing out on big returns" has probably led to worse investment decisions than any other single factor. If a particular asset class, strategy or fund has done very well for three or four years, we know one thing for sure: we should have invested three or four years ago. Now, however, the particular cycle that led to this great performance may be near its end. Smart money is moving, and stupid money is pouring out. Stick to the investment plan and rebalance, which is the exact opposite of the performance chase.

What is rebalancing?

Rebalancing is the process of returning the portfolio to its target asset allocation as outlined in the investment plan. Rebalancing is difficult because it forces you to sell the asset class that performs well and buys more of your worst performing asset classes. This type of countered action is not easy for many investors. Also, rebalancing isn't profitable to the point where it pays off spectacularly (think about U.S. stocks in the late 1990s) and underperforming assets start to take off.

Such a portfolio that allows market returns to move, ensures that asset classes are overweight at market peaks and underweight at market lows - a formula for poor performance. The solution? A rigorous and constant rebalancing.

Don't consider your risk aversion

Don't lose sight of your risk tolerance or your ability to take risks. If you're the type of investor who can't handle the volatility and ups and downs associated with the stock market, perhaps it would be better to invest in the blue-chip stock of an established company rather than the volatile stock of a start-up.

Remember that the expected return carries a risk. If an investment offers very attractive returns, look at its risk profile as well and see how much money you could lose if things go wrong. And don't invest more than you can afford to lose.

A time horizon that is too short or non-existent

Additionally, do not invest without a time horizon in mind. If your goal is to accumulate money to buy a home, it may be more than a medium-term time horizon. If, instead, you are putting your money into the market with the goal of financing a child's college education, it is more of a long-term investment. You will need to find investments that fit your time horizon.

If you've been saving for retirement for 30 years, what the stock market does this year or next shouldn't be your biggest concern. Even if you are about to retire at 70, your life expectancy is probably between 15 and 20 years. If you plan to leave some assets to your heirs, then your time horizon is even longer. Of course, if you are saving for your daughter's college education and she is a secondary school, then your time horizon is appropriately short and your asset allocation should reflect this fact. In general, however, most investors are too focused on the short term.

2. Do not use Stop-Loss orders

If you are not using stop-loss is a clear sign that you do not have a trading plan. Stop-loss orders are generally limited before the losses become substantial. Although there is a risk that a stop order on long positions may be implemented at levels well below those specified if security gaps are reduced, the benefits of such orders outweigh this risk. Often a trader also makes another fairly common mistake, when he cancels a stop order on a loss-making trade just before it can be triggered, because he believes that the security could immediately reverse the course and allow the trade to succeed again.

3. Leaving support for losses

One of the hallmarks of successful traders is their ability to quickly take a small loss if a trade fails and move on to the next trading idea. On the other hand, unsuccessful traders can get paralyzed if a trade goes against them. Rather than acting quickly to make up for a loss, they may remain in a losing position in hopes that the trade will eventually resolve. A losing trade can tie uptrading capital for a long time and can result in increasing losses and severe capital drain.

4. Calculation of the average

Brokerage on a long position in blue-chip stocks may work for an investor who has a long investment horizon, but it can be

fraught with danger for a trader who is trading volatile and riskier stocks.

It is well known that many of the biggest trading losses in history occurred because a trader continued to add a losing position, and was eventually forced to cut the entire position when the magnitude of the loss became unsustainable. Traders are also below conservative investors and tend to average, as security is advancing rather than decreasing. This is an equally risky move that is another common mistake made by a novice trader.

The importance of accepting losses

Too often investors do not accept the simple fact that they are human beings and prone to making mistakes, just like big investors do. If you have made a purchase of shares in a hurry or one of your long-standing large earnings has suddenly taken a turn for the worse, the best thing you can do is accept it. One of the worst things a trader can do is to let his pride take priority over his portfolio and to hold on to an investment at a loss. Or even worse, buy more shares of the stock, since it is now much cheaper.

This is a very common mistake and those who make it do so by comparing the current stock price with the stock's 52-week high. Many people who use this gauge assume that a lapsed stock price represents a good buy. But the fact that a company's stock price increased 30% last year won't help it make more money this year. That's why it pays to analyze why a stock has fallen.

<u>Understanding the fundamentals and false buy signals</u>

Determination of fundamentals, the resignation of a chief executive officer (CEO), or increased competition are all possible reasons for a lower share price; but these same reasons also provide good clues to suspect that the stock may not rise anytime soon. A company may be worth less today but for fundamental reasons. It is important to always have a critical eye, because a low share price could be a false purchase signal.

Be careful to buy shares that look like just a bargain. In many cases, there is a strong underlying reason for a fall in prices. Do your homework and analyze the prospects of a stock before investing in it. You want to invest in companies that will experience sustained growth in the future.

Remember that a company's future operating performance has nothing to do with the price at which you bought its shares. When there is a sharp drop in the price of your shares, try to determine the reasons for the change and see if the company is a good investment for the future. If it is not, transfer your money to a company with better prospects.

5. Too much margin

Margin - the use of borrowed money to buy stocks - can help you earn more, but it can also exaggerate your losses, which makes it potentially detrimental. The worst thing you can do as a new investor is getting carried away by what looks like free money. If you use margin and your investment doesn't go as planned, you eventually find yourself in big debt for nothing. Ask yourself if you want to buy a stocks with your

credit card. Sure, you wouldn't. Excessive use of margin is essentially the same thing, albeit probably at a lower interest rate.

Additionally, using margin requires you to monitor positions much more closely due to the exaggerated gains and losses that accompany small moves in the price. If you don't have the time or knowledge to keep an eye on and make decisions about your positions, and their values go down, your brokerage firm will sell your stock to recoup any accumulated losses.

Since you are a novice investor, use the margin sparingly, if possible, and only if you understand all its aspects and dangers. It can force you to sell all your positions downwards, where you should be in the market for the big breakthrough.

Learn about leverage

According to a well-known investment cliché, leverage is a double-edged sword because it can increase returns on profitable trades and exacerbate losses if trades are lost. Beginner traders may be dazzled by the degree of leverage they hold, especially in forex (FX), but they may soon find that excessive leverage can destroy trading capital in a flash. Attention: if you use a leverage ratio of 50: 1, which is not difficult to find in retail forex trading, a negative move of 2% is enough to wipe out the capital. Brokers must tell traders that more than three-quarters of traders lose money due to the complexity of the market and the negative side of leverage.

6. Follow the flock of sheep blindly

Another common mistake of new entrants is that they blindly follow the pack; as such, they may end up paying too much for hot stocks or they may start short positions in stocks that have already plummeted and may be on the verge of reversing. While experienced traders follow the saying the trend is your friend, they are used to doing business when they are too crowded. New traders, however, can remain in a trading position long after the smart currency has exited it. Beginning traders may also not be sure to take a contrarian approach when required.

Remember: don't put all your eggs in one basket

Diversification is one way to avoid overexposure to any investment. Having a portfolio consisting of multiple investments protects you if one of them loses money. It also helps protect against volatility and extreme price movements in any investment.

Many studies have shown that most managers and mutual funds underperform their benchmarks. In the long run, low- cost index funds typically perform in the top second quartile or above 65% -75% of actively managed funds. Despite all the evidence in favor of indexation, the desire to invest with active managers remains strong. John Bogle, the founder of Vanguard, says it's because: "Hope is eternal, indexing is a little boring, it flies in the face the American way [that]" I can do better ".

Index all or a large portion (70% -80%) of your traditional investment classes. If you can't resist the excitement of pursuing the next great performer, then set aside about 20% - 30% of each asset class for active managers. This could satisfy your desire to pursue outperformance without devastating your portfolio.

7. Do your homework

New traders are often guilty of not doing their homework or not conducting proper research before they start trading. Doing your homework is critical because novice traders don't have the knowledge of seasonal trends or data release times and trading patterns that experts have. For a person who has recently started trading the impulse to trade often exceeds the need to undertake some research, but this can ultimately result in an expensive lesson.

It is a mistake not to research an investment that interests you. Research helps you understand a financial instrument and know what you are in. If you are investing in stocks, for example, do some research about the company and its business plans. Do not act on the premise that markets are efficient and you cannot make money by identifying good investments. Even if this is not an easy task and every other investor has access to the same information you have, it is possible to identify good investments by doing the research.

Don't buy relying on unfounded advice

It is very likely that many people make this mistake at one time or another in their careers as investors. You may hear your relatives or friends talking about a stock they have heard about buying, making skyrocketing profits or releasing a revolutionary new product soon. Even if these things are true, it does not necessarily mean that the stock is "the next big thing" and that you should rush to your online brokerage account to place a purchase order.

Other unfounded suggestions come from television and social media investment professionals who often claim a specific stock as if it were a must buy, but in reality, it's just the flavor of the day. These stock market tips often don't pop up and go straight down after you buy them. Remember, buying media advice is often founded on nothing more than a speculative bet.

This is not to say that you should stop at every stock market tip. If one really gets your attention, the first thing to do is to consider the source. The next thing is to do your homework so that you know what you are buying and why. For example, buying a tech stock with proprietary technology should be based on whether it is the right investment for you, not just what a mutual fund manager said in a media interview.

The next time you're tempted to buy based on a suggestion, don't do it until you have all the data and are comfortable with the company. Ideally, get a second opinion from other impartial investors or financial advisors.

Do not pay too much attention to financial media

Often there is almost nothing in financial news that can help you achieve your goals. There are few newsletters that can provide you with anything of value. Even if there are, how do you identify them in advance?

If someone had useful stock market advice, trading tips or a secret formula to earn a lot of money, would they send it on TV or sell it for $49 a month? No. They would keep their mouths shut, make millions and wouldn't need to sell a newsletter to make a living. The solution? Spend less time watching financial programs on TV and reading newsletters and spend more time creating and sticking to your investment plan.

Face the big picture when buying a stock

For a long-term investor, one of the most important, but often overlooked, things to do is qualitative analysis, or look at the big picture. Bothering one of the best investors, Peter Lynch, once said he found the best investments by looking at his children's toys and the trends they would face. The brand name is also very valuable. Think about how almost everyone in the world knows Coca-Cola; the financial value of the name alone is therefore measured in billions of dollars. Whether it's iPhone or Big Mac, no one can stand in the way of real life.

So pouring budgets or trying to identify buying and selling opportunities with complex technical analysis can work for a long time, but if the world is changing against your company, sooner or later you will lose. Remember that in the late 1980s, a typewriter company could have outperformed any company in its industry, but once personal computers started to become commonplace, a typewriter investor of that era would have done well to assess the big picture and wander around.

Evaluating a company from a qualitative point of view is as important as looking at its sales and earnings. Qualitative analysis is one of the easiest and most effective strategies to evaluate a potential investment.

8. Don't trade on multiple markets

Beginner traders may tend to float from market to market, i.e. from stocks to options, currencies, commodity futures and so on. Operating in many markets can be a great distraction and can prevent the novice trader from gaining the necessary experience to excel in a market.

9. Don't forget about taxes

Keep the tax consequences in mind before investing. You will get a tax deduction on some investments such as municipal bonds. Before investing, look at what your return will be after adjusting your taxes, taking into account the investment, tax bracket and investment time horizon.

Do not pay more than necessary for trading and brokerage fees. By keeping your investment and not trading frequently, you will save on brokerage costs. Finally, look for a broker who does not charge excessive commissions, so that you can maintain a higher return on your investment.

10.   The danger of Hubris

Trading is a very demanding occupation, but the "beginner's luck" experienced by some novice traders can lead them believe that trading is the proverbial road to fast riches. Such overconfidence is dangerous as it breeds complacency and encourages excessive risk-taking that could culminate in a commercial disaster.

It is easy to see from numerous studies that most managers will often fail to achieve their benchmarks. It is not easy to select the managers who outperform in advance. We also know that very few people can profit from time to market in the long term. So why do many investors trust their ability to time the market and/or select the best performing managers? Loyalty guru Peter Lynch once observed: "There are no market timers in the Forbes 400.

Inexperienced day trading

If you insist on becoming an active trader, think twice before trading every day. Day trading can be a dangerous game and should only be attempted by experienced investors. Surely a successful trader, as well as working smart, can gain an advantage by having access to special equipment that is less easily available to the average trader. Did you know that the average daily workstation (with software) can cost tens of thousands of dollars? You will also need a significant amount of trading money to maintain an efficient day trading strategy.

The need for speed is the main reason why you cannot effectively start day trading with the extra $5,000 in your bank account. However, online broker systems are often not fast enough to serve the real day trader; literally, cents per share can make the difference between a profitable trade and a loser. Most brokers recommend that investors take daily trading courses before they start.

Unless you have experience, a platform, and access to fast order execution, think twice before trading daily. If you are not very good at managing risk and stress, there are better options for an investor who is looking to create wealth.

<u>Underestimate your abilities</u>

Some investors, however, tend to believe that they will never excel in investing because they believe that the success of the stock market is reserved only for sophisticated investors. This perception has no truth. While commission fund sellers will probably tell you otherwise, most professional fund managers don't even vote, and the vast majority have underperformed the broad market. With a little time devoted to learning and research, investors can become well equipped to control their portfolios and investment decisions while still being profitable. Remember, many investments stick to common sense and rationality.

Individual investors, for their part, do not have to face the liquidity challenges and overheads of large institutional investors. Any small investor with a sound investment strategy has an equally good chance of beating the market, if not better than so-called investment gurus. Do not assume that you will not be able to successfully participate in the financial markets just because you have a day job.

Conclusions

If you have the money to invest and you can avoid these beginner mistakes, you could charge for your investments; and getting a good return on your investments could bring you closer to your financial goals.

With the tendency of the stock market to produce high gains (and losses), there is no shortage of bad advice and irrational decisions.

Remember, if you are trying to make a big win by betting your money according to your instincts, try a casino. Be proud of your investment decisions and, in the long term, your portfolio will grow to reflect the strength of your actions.

CHAPTER EIGHT
FIVE GOOD REASON TO DAY TRADING

Online trading has seen an increase in popularity in recent years, a growth also due to the increasingly accessible, simple and usable trading platforms even on smartphones and tablets.

More and more people are starting to trade in their free time with the aim of earning a little more every day. Trading can be the tool to get a second income, or in many cases even as a main activity, a living from trading is possible.

1) Become a financially independent trader

Going on your own at 50 is certainly more difficult than at 30 rather than 20, but with a little study, patience and great passion, I can tell you that it can be done. The road to economic independence can be reached even at 60, but it must be strongly desired. What to say, better to know that there are possibilities to do it, and we will go to see them in this article, than to get depressed and feel sorry for yourself without doing anything constructive. Before starting, I wanted to make a talk about passion. Here we are going to talk about financial markets and how to exploit them, a subject that for many of you may at first glance be boring, but when you understand that it is possible to create a respectable economic position at any age, understanding how to exploit the financial markets, I guarante that the passion comes.

Being independent is a bit everyone's dream and online trading, being to all effects an entrepreneurial activity, allows you to set up on your own and manage your business independently. An independent trader is an entrepreneur who has decided to start his own business by investing in the financial markets.

Online trading is a high-risk business, it is true, but not less than any other business. Every entrepreneur when opening any business must take into account that there are risks. The important thing is to know how to manage these risks and in online trading this is possible and it is the fundamental aspect to learn when deciding to trade online.

Generally many kids who stop studying early or who have finished their studies and try their hand at online trading fail for the simple fact that they consider trading an easy way to make money. In trading, actually, if you're not careful it's so easy to make money but it's even easier to lose it. The approach is fundamental. I repeat, it must be an entrepreneurial approach.

Before opening any business, you always look at what are the expenses and what may be the possible earnings to see it is really worth coming across this experience. An entrepreneur who decides to open a shop must start investing by buying goods in order to resell them and must estimate that part of the goods will not be sold with great probability. Therefore he must estimate that the earnings he will have to obtain from the sale will also have to take charge of the unsold to be profitable.

There is also the risk that the unsold may be greater than expected and therefore you can go at a loss. But a true entrepreneur does not stop and optimizes investments in order to make sure that the earnings exceed the expenses and thus grow with his business.

So it must be in trading. You analyze the markets, you see where you can have good margins and where any losses can be contained and you start investing. You can close your investment at any time. It is not certain that every investment must necessarily close in profit. To earn, you also need to know when it is the right time to exit a trade and focus your attention on other assets, on other markets that can be more profitable at that precise moment.

How do you do it? You have to study. The markets are analyzed and based on their trend, the learned trading strategies are applied which, like a dress, must be sewn on each asset. As traders, we must adapt to the markets and follow their curves. We must never make the mistake of thinking that it is the market that must adapt to our strategies, otherwise we will be screwed.

2) Work wherever you want

Working from home, or wherever you want, is the choice that day after day is made by many people who, rather than getting up early in the morning to go to an office every single day of their life, choosing comfort and saving their physical energy.

In fact, nowadays, the web offers various opportunities to earn money online while comfortably seated on the armchair at home in total relaxation.

From home you have the possibility to manage your work in the way you prefer, because you will establish the best hours to work from home in a completely autonomous way and you can choose when to take a day off without being accountable to anyone.

Among the activities that allow you to work independently is online trading. Who decides to become a trader must know that it is a real profession.

Therefore, to trade it is necessary to study a lot and practice as well. If you want to make a profit, you absolutely cannot improvise as a trader, but you need to put the different trading strategies into practice.

3) The benefits of diversifying investments

When trading online we recommend that you diversify your investments across a range of different markets in order to minimize your risk exposure.

If you decide to export heavily and the market moves strongly against you, your potential losses could be huge. However, by differentiating your exposure across multiple open positions, you reduce the impact that a large market event can significantly impact your overall profit margins.

When trading online you can easily control and manage your investments to build a diversified portfolio that offers consistent returns.

4) Opportunity at any time

Markets can move quickly in both directions, there are opportunities at any time of the day or night; thanks to modern and reliable mobile trading platforms it will be easier to trade at the best time. Choose a broker that has a mobile application that allows you to manage your account via smartphone, tablet or PC.

5) Money always safe and secure

If you choose to start trading, choose a broker that is reliable, regulated, whose funds are safe and secure.

This is sometimes a difficult choice as it is not possible to know everything and the search is sometimes complicated and long.

CHAPTER NINE
WHY DO MOST ASPIRING TRADERS FAIL?

You may not have believed that an online trading book could tell you this much...but here's the truth: it has been estimated that 90% of aspiring traders will blow their capital up within the first year of business. This data could create dismay in traders or potential interested parties; but go ahead with the reading to understand how this is possible.

The question that arises is: why does this happen? Is trading so difficult that only a select few can succeed? The answer is no; everyone can potentially be good traders but under specific conditions.

Here is the classic story of many improvised traders: maybe it can happen that the first trades are lucky. We think we have already understood everything and we begin to increase the size of the positions. At some point comes a large unexpected loss that halves your capital. The impromptu trader tries to recover everything immediately. However, things no longer work as they did in the beginning and the capital continues to decrease until it is inexorably zero.

This is a stereotypical scenario but not very far from reality. The problem is that very often beginners throw themselves into the market with large sums of money, in a hurry to make substantial profits without really knowing what they are doin

There are many other profitable professions in the world: lawyer, banker, doctor, etc. However, these professions require several years of study and practice before obtaining an important economic return. So why should trading be any different? Trading is a profession like any other. It can be carried out not as a main occupation (to have an extra income compared to a "classic job"); in any case, however, it is necessary to study and acquire specific knowledge. Fortunately, becoming a successful trader can take a lot less than the path it takes to become a doctor or an engineer. A lot of study and a lot of practice, however, are the same fundamental requirements to be a good trader.

Don't be in a hurry: the market continually offers good opportunities. In the world of trading, the saying "every left over is lost" is the most wrong thing that can exist. It is good to know first what you are doing: practice trading using a demo account and, only after you are confident enough in your strategy and skills, you can think about using part of your capital.

When starting with real money it is important to start with caution by opening small positions. The key point is not to win very quickly, but to stay in the game long enough to really know how to move and really start earning.

There are three basic concepts that an aspiring trader must absolutely know before starting. They are very simple concepts that we have decided to summarize in a formula to always keep in mind.

1) Strict method:

It is important to choose a strategy that is suitable for your trading style (we will talk about this in the following articles) and to stick to the strategy without inventing. Trading is a systematic business; trusting an intuition can lead to some lucky wins but it doesn't work in the long run.

2) Money management:

Managing your capital is essential. The key to trading success is to keep your capital whatever happens. We will go into more detail in this topic but it is essential to understand the right balance between maximizing profit and keeping risk under control. Only good money management will allow you to make the success of your trading strategy bear fruit.

2. Cold Mind:

Trading psychology is an underestimated aspect but it is very important. When there is money at stake, stress increases, compromising our lucidity in making decisions. There is a tendency to close profitable positions early to make a quick profit. On the contrary, we tend to leave losing positions open for too long in the hope of being able to recover. This causes winnings to be less than losses and in the long run this destroys the trader's capital. Trading psychology is important to be able to implement your strategy without greed or fear. The good trader learns to trust his system after the "defeats"; in the same way he knows how not to get too carried away even after many "victories"

CHAPTER TEN

THE BEST TRADERS IN THE WORLD

Getting to know who the best traders in the world are can not only satisfy your curiosity, but if you are working or approaching the online trading sector it can be an option to have points of reference from which to draw inspiration and learn.

Of course, no novice trader can think of joining the best professionals in the world, nevertheless having the opportunity to learn from the best traders can be very useful.

Who are the best traders in the world?

Being among the best traders does not necessarily correspond to being the richest.

In fact, the best are those who have managed to make history, not only for the earnings obtained, but also for the great skills demonstrated.

It goes without saying, however, that often the two lines correspond, and mostly they are investors who have made their way through their methods.

For this reason, among the best traders in the world there are investors who are often mentioned on TV or in newspapers, and not necessarily only in the financial sect

The best traders in the world are:

Warren Buffett

Also known as the Oracle of Omaha, Warren Buffett is a true legend.

Only a single person can own as many as seven investment funds since the 1960s.

The creation of the Berkshire Hathaway fund, the fund with which Buffett has stakes everywhere, is certainly what made him go down in history.

Warren Buffett's input has always been to invest in companies that are understated and that have especially long-term potential.

Buffett is rated as the best trader of all time.

Among the most important investments made by Buffet there is necessarily the one made in Coca-Cola.

George Soros

He is also on the list of the best traders in the world.

Shares represent one of the best known, appreciated and always used investments by savers.

Today the name of Soros is also and above all recognized for events that not only concern finance but also politics and society.

Soros' success is all based on the Soros Fund Management investment fund, a fund dedicated to speculation on upcoming bursts of financial bubbles.

In practice, it was through this fund that Soros made stratospheric gains by betting, for example, on the collapse of the pound in 1992, the collapse of our Lira and the fall in price of the Swiss Franc.

However, Soros' speculations have not always translated into earnings, but today his financial assets are calculated above 19 billion dollars, which also makes him fall into the category of the richest traders in the world.

James Simons

James Simons is certainly one of the most talented and capable traders to enter the history of online trading, although not among the richest.

The reason that led him to be among the best is characteristic.

Simons, in fact, was one of the first investors to adopt mathematics to finance.

His investment fund is all about mathematical models.

But Simons is also part of the history of the best traders in the world for having predicted the subprime mortgage crisis and for having used short positions on stocks at the right time.

John Paulson

John Paulson is the Founder of the Paulson & Co.

With his nickname, The Sultan of Subprime, Paulson made it into the books of trading history.

In fact, Paulson was the trading genius who most of all managed to anticipate the subprime crisis.

Thanks to short selling, in the middle of the subprime crisis, Paulson was able to multiply the capital of his funds by up to 2500 percent.

Steven Cohen

Also called the lord of the hundred thousand dollars a day, Steven Cohen must necessarily be included among the best traders in the world.

In fact, this trader's earnings when he worked as a broker at Gruntal & Co.

Short selling of shares is the secret of its success.

It was thanks to the gains made through shorts that Cohen was able to enter the top ten of traders.

The richest traders in the world

As we have mentioned, the best are not always necessarily the richest.

In fact, among those we have indicated among the richest there is only George Soros.

According to the latest data, in addition to Soros, the richest traders in the world are:

Martin Schwartz

Day trading professor Martin Schwartz made his fortune as quickly as it was surprising.

According to some estimates, Schwartz is now able to earn around seventy thousand dollars every day.

A large part of his success is linked to his proverbial ability to use futures.

Stanley Druckenmiller

While having no background in the world of finance, Drockenmiller was able to earn something like $ 3.5 billion during his career.

This investor has managed to become one of the richest traders in the world using a methodology focused on the concept of top down.

A shrewd and scrupulous study of the economic environment and of the famous reference context within which he used to insert the most classic technical analysis.

Day Trading

Alexander Elder

Alexander Elder is not only one of the richest traders in the world but he is also one of the most followed by all investors.

With so many books and interventions, Elder's advice is considered very valid by most traders around the world.

Elder is identified as one of the greatest experts in technical analysis and market psychology.

Larry Hite

Larry Hite's name is linked to the development of the most important trading community in the world.

Larry Hite is very productive in training.

Larry's advice, like Elder's, is also found to be very useful and has a huge following from industry users around the world.

CHAPTER ELEVEN
THE STRATEGIS OF THE GREATS

Warren Buffett's strategies

In-depth description of Warren Buffett's strategies, which will make you invest in the stock market with criteria, imitating the choices of a character who dominated the market in the new millennium.

If you have no idea who we are talking about, we advise you to pay close attention to the premise on the companies that have made Warren Buffett known, with the aim of making you understand how precious the tips on the approach to investments in the stock market can be provided by such a industry expert.

According to many, he is the largest value investor ever. According to Forbes he was the richest man in the world in 2007 and 2008 and is currently firmly in the top ten. In short, here's who Warren Buffett is and why everyone should follow the advice offered by the Omaha economist. Born 85 years ago, still today without rivals at its height when it comes to finding the most appropriate way to invest in the stock market and earn impressive figures. Even if we talk about charity, Buffet has proved to be a great man that many should take as an example, having donated a

whopping 37 billion dollars to the populations of the Third World and pledging to allocate 83% of his total wealth to the Bill & Melinda Gates Foundation.

Warren Buffett's ten strategies

Investing in the stock market in the best way, here are the ten strategies that Warren Buffett uses when dealing with important decisions. Widespread a few years ago, they still occupy a very important role even today for investors who choose the most modern trading routes to make their money grow.

1. Invest based on your knowledge

If you don't know a market well, Warren Buffett advises you to change your lens and not get carried away by the desire to try always and in any case. Even if you are based on successful forecasting methods, the most appropriate choice is always to refer to personal knowledge brands, such as companies whose information is known through their work.

2. Yes to long-term investments

Warren Buffett does not pay attention to what happens in the short term, but rather advises users to thoroughly study the trends relating to at least the last ten years, before making a long-term investment where he even recommends holding the position forever, if possible, just as he did with the Coca-Cola shares he has owned for 27 years.

3. Here are the factors to keep an eye on

Before reserving part of your capital for the shares of a particular company, it is necessary to understand if you can really rely on it without taking too many risks and with an excellent probability of profit. The factors are low debt amounts, a good balance sheet and a sufficiently high price-to- earnings ratio.

4. Approximate management? No thanks

If you have a great opportunity to take home securities at bargain prices, but on the other hand the company that issues them does not reveal real management amounts (keeping vague), the right choice according to Warren Buffett's strategies is changing direction and not risking bankruptcy.

5. Buy at the right time

As Buffet teaches, who in the past has made great deals buying companies in a recession (Bank of America is one of them) it is good to find the right time to make purchases as well as for sales. If others are greedy you need to be afraid, if others are afraid you need greed, says the economist, describing his experience with a sort of proverb.

6. Don't buy everything right away

If following the previous advice you have decided to invest in the stock market considering the shares of a particular company that you consider advantageous, do not immediately rush into the purchase of all the securities by exhausting your available capital. This is because the unexpected is always around the corner and a right intuition could turn into an incredible loss. Warren Buffett teaches that the right method is to invest some of the money in the initial phase, and then analyze the trend and gradually proceed with new purchases in case everything goes as planned.

7. Cash always available

Warren Buffett believes cash reserves are very important in any case, both if we win, and if instead we have to face unpleasant losses, hypotheses always to be considered. In the first case, liquidity would give us the opportunity to increase our investments in a stock (in this regard, we connect to the sixth advice), while in the second it would avoid total disaster if our shares were to take a bad turn.

8. Admit your mistakes

When it comes to investments, it is always hard to admit to yourself that you were wrong to make a prediction and that therefore it is time to look towards new horizons learning from the past. Even Warren Buffett, who we reiterate as one of the richest men in the world, admits he made glaring oversights, such as when he sold Disney shares before a noticeable rise.

9. Also consider foreign securities

Although Buffet admits that investing in the stock market by basing his attention on stocks he knows is the best choice, he adds that the right strategy is to keep an eye on foreign stocks as well. This is because sometimes they can yield more than the internal ones or even compensate for the losses of the latter.

10. Calculate the weight of the tax on profits

The capital gain, that is the capital gain or in simple terms what you go to earn from the difference between the sale and purchase price of a stock, is subject to annoying taxes that limit profits. For this reason, before closing a position in your favor, it is good to calculate how much you are going to earn by removing the amount due to the tax authorities, in order to understand if it is really convenient to close the position. Of course, avoiding commissions will also be an important aspect.

Investing in the stock market like George Soros
Who is George Soros?

George Soros understood how the game works and not just the stock markets but the economy in general. He is ten steps ahead of the others and this explains the results that have always made people talk about himself.

Investing in the stock market is one of the many ways in which "the rich" manage to grow their capital year after year. They defend it from the erosive force of inflation and George Soros has used this and many other tricks to build a boundless empire of wealth.

Soros protected himself from inflation like this

To realize the incessant "hard work" that inflation does on our savings, I'll give you an example.

If inflation is 2.5 percent annually, the purchasing power of your money decreases by the same percentage every year. So if for example this year you buy a pound of platinum for $ 1000, the following year the same pound of platinum will cost you $ 1025. The figures are invented but they give the idea.

<u>The solution to beat inflation</u>

The only solution to this phenomenon is to find a way to make your money grow with a force greater than the one of inflation.

One of these methods is investing in the stock market with a method that guarantees, I repeat, guarantees, the constant increase of your capital over time.

To do this you have to strictly block the losses and let the profits run.

I said strictly since this is a golden rule. This rule is trivialized by most but it is fundamental. This is because if, for example, you force yourself to block your losses at 7 percent and to collect profits only when your stock reaches at least 30 percent, the differential between these two percentages will mathematically guarantee you the increase in capital in the long term.

George Soros made Easy

By taking advantage of the strength of compound interest, your money can be multiplied easily. This force according to Einstein is the most miraculous force of nature. This phrase is well known to Soros and has always been applied by him without exception. We will see our savings increase at a rate comparable to that at which mice reproduce. This is realized by reinvesting the profits made in order to obtain a more and more robust capital.

As the amount of capital invested increases, the speed at which it grows multiplies.

This is another explanation of the immense wealth accumulated by Soros.

This method even works if we assume that we randomly choose the securities we want to invest in. But rest assured that Soros doesn't do that. In fact it will work much more if we respect certain investment criteria. This happens when we use certain (trivial but very effective) tools that can make us find certain titles in a short time and with minimum effort. These are the stocks that can maximize the yield of this strategy.

How does this strategy work?

This Soros taught, but it was not at all easy to understand because the simple is always masked by the complicated. It is necessary to choose stocks with excellent fundamentals that is guided by a management that knows how to make money go well. Over the years, these stocks have seen excellent returns on investment in terms of capital gains and perhaps even dividends distributed to shareholders.

Only a trainer other than the classic ones, able to explain these concepts to you in a very simple way as it should be explained to a child, will clarify how all the premises I have just described can be applied in practice. It is necessary to carry out a rigorous analysis but know that not all rigorous analyzes must necessarily be complicated: rigorous analyzes are such because they are conducted with simple effective criteria and in a very careful way, not because they are complicated to put into practice.

This analysis allows you to compare certain fundamental variables with each other (i.e. that describe the economic characteristics of the Company) in a specific market context and have a fairly precise idea of the financial health conditions of the company you are at a "glance" examining (a more detailed analysis can be obtained by reading the financial statements carefully).

Soros teaches us the importance of the Safety Margin

You need to look for a safety margin that is realized only when you are able to buy a security at a price well below its intrinsic value.

In other words, it is like knowing that a pair of Roberto Cavalli shoes are worth about $ 200 (for how they are made, for the material they choose and for the image impact they give you), you know that they are normally available on the market. for more than $ 400 and you can buy them in an outlet for $ 150: you got a great deal right from the start.

In this case it can be said that you bought with an excellent safety margin.

You have a kind of insurance that guarantees you even in the worst market conditions that your stock will hardly go below the price at which you bought it.

You will also know that since the average market price is around $ 400 with peaks even at $ 500, sooner or later the market (made up of a sometimes very bizarre relationship between supply and demand) will recognize the intrinsic value of that security.

The stop loss

When the stock reaches the maximum price that the market can give it, it is time to take home some of the gains made.

For example, we could collect only the gain made and continue to trust that stock while strictly respecting the Stop Loss at minus 7% (remember that stocks that grow very often continue to grow without stopping).

Then the moment will come when for a stock you invest in, the Stop Loss will be positioned above the price at which you bought it: from this moment on for this stock you will no longer be able to lose, because even if it loses 7%, you will sell at a price higher than the price at which you bought it.

The stop loss is dynamic

This happens because the stop loss is dynamic and is raised as the stock grows in price. In fact, if you imagine buying a stock at 37 dollars and 45 cents, you will initially set a stop loss at 32.55 dollars.

If the stock goes from $ 35 to $ 45, the minus 7 percent stop loss will go from $ 32.55 to $ 41.85 and even if the stock price falls to this level triggering your stop loss, you would still sell for profit, since the price at which you sell (the stop loss in fact) is higher than the price at which you bought it.

You may think that it is not easy to choose stocks that have a good chance of passing this test and giving high returns on your investment: in general it is so because if for example we consider the size of the American market the work you should do to study one for oneself among one all titles is truly monstrous.

But there are tools called Stock Screener which are software that extract you from the "great sea" of the American market (for example and not only) the stocks that reflect certain characteristics you are looking for.

You simply have to specify what characteristics the title you are looking for has and the Stock Screener will return the title or titles that meet the requirements you specify: a bit like agencies for lonely hearts do.

So let's imagine you have the name of the stock you intend to invest in: it's a stock that has a good safety margin and high growth potential.

Soros buys stocks only when the time is right

I understood from Soros that to buy stocks it is always better to wait for the right moment.

This is because the market sometimes makes fluctuations that can penalize the stock you have chosen in the short term (days or months) even if it has excellent characteristics and potential.

This happens because the market has psychological characteristics being made up of people like you, who are in the throes of euphoria on some days and in depression on others.

The study of a stock chart: Soros docet!

Studying the stock chart will help you decide the most profitable time to avoid these short-term penalties.

What I have described to you is the method that real investors follow, those who earn on the stock market constantly and continuously. I have shared these secrets in this course.

Remember that to aim for maximum results you must also take care of your psychology, that's how: you too can join this group if you want to learn how to manage your money autonomously through Investments in Shares but if you still think that Investments in the Stock Exchange are similar to the lottery game and you expect to have results without committing a minimum, then this "adventure" is not for you.

If, on the other hand, you are willing to dedicate yourself to this discipline because you don't like the idea of letting your money rot in the bank or entrust it to people you don't even know, then for you this article can represent the beginning of a path that can give you great satisfaction, both financially and personal

CONCLUSION

If you are reading the conclusion, it means that you have reached the end of the book.

I hope it was a pleasant reading and the content was interesting.

Hope all of this has served to improve your way of trading intraday, but not only that!

I have also tried to help you understand how important it is to have a trading plan, or understand what your goals are or how to best manage risk.

I also hope with this book you will discover the method to make your trading more profitable, but above all, that you will learn the tools to try to safeguard your capital.

As I always say, trading doesn't mean playing in the casino.

Trading has become their job for many, and for some, the possibility that has allowed them to significantly increase their standard of living.

But behind all this there is study, preparation, discipline, organization and above all, never improvisation.

I wish you every success in trading and in other types of business, have a good life